Contents

Overview 3
Introduction 4
1. Disciplinary approaches to how change happens 5
    History 5
    Politics 8
    Sociology 11
    Social anthropology 14
    Psychology 15
    Economics 17
    Management and organisational studies 19
    International relations and globalisation 20
    Geography 21
    Legal studies 22
    Technology and science 24
    Philosophy 25
    Ecology 25
    Cross-disciplinary approaches to how change happens 27
2. The rough guide to how change happens 29
    The rough guide to how change happens 30
    The abolition of the slave trade and slavery in Britain 32
3. Approaches to change in contemporary development thinking 35
    Market liberalisation 35
    Managed markets 36
    Corporate social responsibility 36
    International aid 37
    Empowerment 37
    Grassroots participation and social organisation 38
    Reforming the state 39
    Land reform and securing private property 40
    Changing attitudes and beliefs 41
Conclusions 44
Endnotes 47
References 52

© Oxfam GB 2007

This is a print version of a report originally issued online as *How Change Happens: Interdisciplinary Perspectives for Human Development* at: www.oxfam.org.uk/publications

The online report was uploaded in February 2007

This edition transferred to print-on-demand in 2007

ISBN 978 0 85598 597 4

This publication is copyright, but may be used free of charge for the purposes of advocacy, campaigning, education and research, provided that the source is acknowledged in full. The copyright holder requests that all such use be registered with them for impact assessment purposes. For copying in any other circumstances, or for re-use in other publications, or for translation or adaptation, permission must be secured and a fee may be charged. For permission or further information, please email publish@oxfam.org.uk.

Oxfam GB, founded in 1942, is a development, humanitarian, and campaigning agency dedicated to finding lasting solutions to poverty and suffering around the world. Oxfam believes that every human being is entitled to a life of dignity and opportunity, and it works with others worldwide to make this become a reality.

Oxfam GB is a member of Oxfam International, a confederation of 13 agencies of diverse cultures and languages, which share a commitment to working for an end to injustice and poverty – both in long-term development work and at times of crisis.

For further information about Oxfam's publishing, and online ordering, visit www.oxfam.org.uk/publications.

Roman Krznaric is an independent consultant who specialises in multidisciplinary approaches to issues in human development and social policy. He has degrees in the social sciences and Latin American studies from the universities of Oxford, London, and Essex, where he obtained a Ph.D. in political sociology. He can be contacted at roman.krznaric@gmail.com. Many thanks to the following for their advice and suggestions: Tom Battye, Phil Bloomer, Becky Buell, Rosalind Eyben, Flora Gathorne-Hardy, John Gaventa, Lisa Gormley, Duncan Green, Alex Grigor, Thalia Kidder, Ruth Mayne, Forrest Metz, Annalise Moser, Andrew Ray, Barbara Stocking, Caroline Sweetman, Kevin Watkins, and especially Kate Raworth.

This Oxfam Research Report was written to inform policy development and as a background paper for the Oxfam Poverty Report (forthcoming in 2008). It is published in order to share widely the results of Oxfam-commissioned research. The views expressed in the report are those of the author and do not necessarily reflect Oxfam's views.

For further information on the issues raised in this paper, please e-mail enquiries@oxfam.org.uk or go to www.oxfam.org.uk.

Overview

Has development thinking become too narrow and specialised? Does it fail to draw sufficiently on what has been learned outside the realm of development studies about how social change happens? These are the questions at the centre of this paper. The analysis is divided into three parts. Part 1 is a general survey of approaches to explaining change from the perspective of a wide range of academic disciplines, such as history, politics, psychology, and geography. Part 2 provides a thematic summary of these approaches in the form of a table, 'The rough guide to how change happens', which can be used as a tool to help understand and explain changes that have taken place. A case study of the British struggle against slavery and the slave trade illustrates the utility of the 'rough guide'. Part 3 argues that current developing thinking advocates only a narrow range of approaches to change. The result is that most development strategies are limited in five main ways: they are excessively reformist and insensitive to underlying power and inequality; they largely ignore environmental issues; they overlook the importance of personal relationships and promoting mutual understanding as a strategy of change; they fail to appreciate fully the contextual factors that limit change; and they lack a multidisciplinary agility to draw on the broad range of approaches to change that exist outside the confines of development studies.

Introduction

How change happens is a central issue in almost every field of academic inquiry. Historians debate how National Socialism emerged in Germany. Economists investigate the drivers of economic growth. Sociologists examine the rise of radical Islam. Psychologists discuss the incentive structures that alter human behaviour. Geographers study the role of climate in the rise and fall of civilisations.

Unsurprisingly, there is a wide – and bewildering – range of explanations, ideas, and viewpoints on the general subject of how and why change takes place. So what do we really know about how human societies change? To what extent do strategies to tackle poverty and inequality, and to promote human development, draw upon what has been learned about change in domains of knowledge outside development studies? Has development thinking become too narrow in its approach to change, trapped by specialised knowledge and habitual approaches? These are the questions at the centre of this paper.

The analysis is divided into three parts. Part 1 describes different approaches to how change happens from a variety of disciplinary perspectives. These include, among others, history, politics, sociology, psychology, economics, international relations, legal studies, and ecology. Part 1 addresses the diverse kinds of change that concern each discipline; for instance, political scientists are interested in transformations of political systems, psychologists in individual behaviour, sociologists in worldviews. It highlights the general factors and conceptual frameworks used to explain change, not empirical content.

The second part sets out a tool for thinking about change, drawing on the various perspectives described in Part 1 – in the form of a table called 'The rough guide to how change happens'. It then examines an example of major social change – the abolition of the slave trade and slavery in Britain – which illustrates the utility of the 'rough guide' as a tool for understanding and explaining how change takes place.

The third part of the paper explores the extent to which contemporary development strategies to tackle poverty and inequality employ the full range of approaches to change proposed in the 'rough guide'. It examines strategies such as managing markets, reforming the state, empowerment, and corporate social responsibility, and traces them back to their roots in particular academic disciplines.

I conclude that current development thinking makes use of only a narrow range of possible approaches to change. The result is that development strategies are limited in five main ways: they are excessively reformist and insensitive to underlying power and inequality; they largely ignore environmental issues; they overlook the importance of personal relationships and promoting mutual understanding as a strategy of change; they fail to fully appreciate the contextual factors that limit change; and they lack a multidisciplinary agility to draw on the broad range of approaches to change that exist outside the narrow confines of development studies.

Overall there is a need for broader thinking about how change does happen so that we can be more creative and adept at devising strategies to confront the enormous challenges facing our societies and planet.

Part 1: Disciplinary approaches to how change happens

Before embarking on this interdisciplinary journey, some brief comments are required. I have focused primarily on intellectual trends currently prevalent in Western scholarship. Since it makes little sense to investigate change without taking into account what prevents it, I have, where relevant, also discussed the obstacles to change identified by different academic traditions.

For each discipline there are sections on the most significant approaches, theories, or debates concerning how change happens (for example, the discussion among historians about the relative importance of actors and structures). Where an approach to change arises in more than one discipline, I have discussed it under the discipline where it has been most influential or prevalent (for example, examining change through the eyes and actions of ordinary people rather than élites is common in sociology and oral history, but is most closely associated with social anthropology).

These sections generally address at least one of the four major questions of change that repeatedly occur, both explicitly and implicitly, across disciplines:

- Who or what was involved in the change? (e.g. individual actors or state institutions)
- What strategies were used to bring about the change? (e.g. reformism, mass mobilisation)
- What were the contexts that affected how the change happened? (e.g. urbanisation, power relationships)
- What was the process or pathway of change? (e.g. demonstration effects, cumulative progress)

Keeping these questions in mind will help you navigate through the diverse approaches to change that appear below, and make it easier to compare and contrast different disciplines.

Not all thinking about how change happens fits into standard disciplinary categories, so I have created an additional category of cross-disciplinary approaches. Also, when analysing the various academic approaches to change, I deliberately exclude development studies because it is explored in greater detail in Part 3.

By necessity this is a summary of perspectives and cannot reflect the nuances of thinking about change in each academic discipline. The intention is to be suggestive rather than exhaustive, to raise questions rather than provide all the answers.

History

'The study of history is a study of causes', wrote E. H. Carr in *What is History?*[1] More than most other thinkers, historians have endeavoured to explain why things happen. They are interested in the relationship between continuity and change. As such, history provides an ideal starting point for this paper. How have historians approached the issue of how change happens?

Actors and structures

The first area of debate is the relative importance of actors and structures. Until the mid twentieth century, change was largely attributed to individual actors, particularly heroic or powerful figures. The military strategy of Napoleon or Churchill was considered responsible for the course of wars and the fate of nations. An exemplary work in this tradition is the *Letters and Speeches of Oliver Cromwell* (1845) by Thomas Carlyle, in which he depicts Cromwell as a heroic leader struggling against the social turbulence of his time. 'History', said Carlyle, 'is the biography of great men'.[2]

An opposing approach, which developed with the rise of Marxist interpretations of history that become prominent in the 1960s, is that changes in economic and social structures are responsible for major historical shifts.[3] For example, as a country industrialises, the owners of industrial capital become more economically powerful, which translates into political power. They are more easily able to impose their interests on society, for instance by ensuring tax laws are to their benefit. This type of analysis derives from Marx's view that 'dominant material relationships' are more important than ideas in changing society.[4] As Eric Hobsbawm points out in his essay 'What do historians owe to Karl Marx?',[5] the rise of economic and social history reflects the general acceptance of this approach by historians of many political persuasions. However, the deterministic aspects of Marx's theory have not had broad appeal.

Class and other social groups

An element of the Marxist perspective described above is the idea that history changes because of changes in class structure and interrelations. In Marx's *The 18th Brumaire of Louis Bonaparte* (1852), he analyses how the 1848 revolution in France failed because the industrial-financial bourgeoisie and the landed aristocracy united in the Party of Order to defeat the proletarian class.[6] This form of analysis remains common among contemporary historical sociologists. In *Capitalist Development and Democracy* (1992), a study focusing on Western Europe, Latin America, and the Caribbean, Dietrich Reuschmeyer, Evelyne Huber Stephens, and John D. Stephens argue that the growth of a working class, divisions between urban and rural economic élites, and weakening of the landowning class, have been fundamental for the emergence of liberal democracy. These conditions are unlikely to emerge in countries with limited economic development, resulting in the continuity of practices such as labour-repressive agriculture and oligarchic politics.[7]

Since the 1980s, class analysis has waned in popularity. Under the influence of disciplines such as sociology, historians have increasingly focused on alternative personal identities such as ethnicity and gender to help explain change. In *A People's History of the United States* (1995), Howard Zinn shows how African-Americans and women have shaped the country's history as much as organised labour. Studies such as Elizabeth Wayland Barber's *Women's Work: The First Twenty Thousand Years* (1994) have helped transform the subject matter of labour history. The importance of gendered perspectives on history and social change is evident in the emergence of academic fields such as women's history, gender studies, and feminist economics (see below).

Above and below

Until the 1960s most history was written 'from above'. It was the history of kings and queens, aristocrats, parliaments, political parties, laws, and the upper echelons of ecclesiastical hierarchies. This approach – that history was, and should be, made by élites – is associated with the early twentieth-century historian Lewis Namier, a conservative with a strong distaste for, and fear of, social change.[8] A model of change associated with the history 'from above' school is that social change filters from the top down. An example concerns the shift in late medieval Europe from the pervasive use of violence to resolve social conflict, to more conciliatory methods involving dialogue and other non-violent means. Norbert Elias has described this as a 'civilizing process' which spread throughout society from its origins in the European upper classes.[9]

In history written 'from above' there was little conception that everyday people were important historical actors. This changed with the advent of historical analysis 'from below'. In *The Making of the English Working Class* (1963), an account of artisan and working-class society between 1780 and 1832, E. P. Thompson specifically set out 'to rescue the poor stockinger, the Luddite cropper, the 'obsolete' hand-loom weaver, the 'utopian' artisan, and even the deluded follower of Joanna Southcott, from the enormous condescension of posterity'.[10] Similarly, Christopher Hill's *The World Turned Upside Down: Radical Ideas During the English Revolution* (1972) helped turn historiography upside down by examining popular revolt in seventeenth-century England by previously little-known groups such as the Diggers and Ranters. In *Memoria del Fuego* (*Memory of Fire*, 1982–1986), a narrative history of the Americas, Uruguayan intellectual Eduardo Galeano showed that social change was a product of both colonial repression and resistance from below, be it individual acts of heroism or mass revolutionary movements. Accompanying the rise of history from below was the growth of studies on the history of grassroots social movements, and oral history (see the section below on sociology). This shifted the causes of historical change from the realm of traditional political, economic, and religious institutions to 'the common people'.

Internal and external

Historians have been concerned with whether change comes from within or without the entity being analysed, such as a nation-state or an empire. The final volume of Edward Gibbon's *Decline and Fall of the Roman Empire* (1788) identifies four major causes of the ruin of Rome, which operated over a one-thousand-year period. Among the four was a largely external cause (the hostile attacks of barbarians) and an internal cause (the domestic quarrels of the Romans). The analysis of internal and external causes is also common in politics, sociology, international relations, and economics.

Cycles and crises

Several classical historians devised cyclical theories of history. They argued that civilisations passed through periods of birth, growth, and decay: the evolution of society mirrored evolution in nature. In his *History*, the ancient Greek historian Polybius, drawing on Aristotle's analysis of regime change, argued that monarchy naturally turns into tyranny, which transforms into aristocracy, which degenerates into oligarchy, which produces democracy, which leads to mob rule. Historical change was seen to be governed by such natural laws. The importance of cycles has filtered into many other disciplines, evident in theories of economic cycles, social-movement cycles, and electoral cycles.

In contrast to the idea of 'natural' cycles, some historians have invoked specific junctures or crises to explain change. The role of women in the First World War in Britain, for instance as munitions workers, gave a significant boost not only to women's future involvement in the workplace, but also to movements to gain voting rights for women. Constitutional change was 'intimately bound up with the impact of war'.[11] That is, change is not only a product of long-term transformations of social and economic structures; it also emerges during periods of flux or dislocation that provide unexpected openings. The importance of key junctures and crises as potential moments of change was theorised in Antonio Gramsci's *Prison Notebooks*, written in the early 1930s, partly based on his study of nineteenth-century Italian history.[12] A related idea is that history changes through cataclysmic events rather than through longer-term catalysts. For example, the assassination of the Archduke Franz Ferdinand is often considered a cataclysmic occurrence that sparked the beginning of the First World War.

Chance and natural causes

Not all historical change is seen as intentional or a product of human societies. Gibbon's explanation of the decline of the Roman Empire placed considerable emphasis on the role of natural disasters such as floods and damage caused by fires. Gibbon also allowed accident or chance to play a part in his analysis. When discussing how Bajazet was deterred from marching into Central Europe by an attack of gout, he wrote that 'an acrimonious humour falling on a single fibre of one man may prevent or suspend the misery of nations'.[13] By the mid twentieth century historians had become less convinced that chance played a central part in change, evident in the view expressed by E. H. Carr in the 1960s that 'the role of accident in history is nowadays seriously exaggerated'.[14]

Reform and revolution

Historians distinguish whether change takes place through evolutionary processes of slow, gradual reform and transformation, or through the more rapid, dynamic, and extreme revolutionary overthrow of institutions and imposition of new social and political orders. There is a significant strand of thinking in British historiography supporting the view that gradual reform has been the 'natural' form of historical change in the country, and that the British are not a 'revolutionary people'. This view has been disputed by historians such as Christopher Hill who argued that the country's revolutionary activities and episodes have been unjustifiably neglected by historians.

Reform or revolution is also a central issue of strategies of change. Rosa Luxemburg's pamphlet *Social Reform or Revolution* (1900) argued that social democratic reform was an ineffective means of fundamentally ameliorating the conditions of poor workers. The ruling classes and politicians could not be trusted to enact change. This theme is echoed in Franz Fanon's study of decolonisation, *The Wretched of the Earth* (1963), which advocated revolutionary anti-colonial movements that changed social structures from the bottom up through the use of violence.[15] Reformists have been much more optimistic about the possibilities of working within existing institutions to achieve change. This might require lobbying governments, forming political parties, and making alliances with progressive elements among ruling élites. An example is the gradual integration of the German Green Party into the mainstream of the political system.

Politics

Politics developed as an independent academic discipline in the late nineteenth century, when it became increasingly clear that the political institutions and processes of nation-states were developing autonomy from traditional social, economic, and religious organisations and systems. A consequence was that the activities of states and governments grew in importance as variables in explaining change.

Institutional analysis

Political analysts generally assume that a society changes when its political institutions change. It has been common to emphasise that alterations in the balance and separation of powers between the executive, legislature, judiciary, bureaucracy, and military can have significant consequences. For instance, excessive executive power vested in presidents can contribute to the emergence of dictatorship. A classic text on these themes is Montesquieu's *The Spirit of the Laws* (1748).

Political science has also been devoted to the role of elections and electoral systems as causes of change. The kind of government that voters have elected (usually understood to lie somewhere on a uni-dimensional left–right spectrum) strongly influences the nature and extent of change that takes place. On a more systemic level, a first-past-the-post electoral system can bring social and political stability, whereas a proportional representation system can result in fragmentation of the party system and ineffective coalition governments (although it may provide more effective representation). Forms of political participation (such as direct democracy through referenda or indirect democracy through electing constituency representatives) also affect what kind of change can take place. There has been a resurgence of institutional analysis since the 1980s, sometimes referred to as the 'new institutionalism', where there is discussion of how to 'design' political institutions to achieve certain outcomes. An important text of this kind is Arend Lijphart's *Democracies: Patterns of Majoritarian and Consensus Government in Twenty-one Countries* (1984).

Many such institutional approaches have been criticised for depicting the modern state as a neutral 'place' where politics happens, rather than an entity that reflects and embodies the configuration of power in society (see the section below on sociology). This is usually described as a 'classical pluralist' theory of the state, where it is assumed that states are highly responsive to pressure from various organised groups in society but none of them enjoy special privileges or influence.[16] In contrast, Michael Mann's *The Sources of Social Power: The Rise of Classes and Nation States* (1985), conceives of states as containing 'polymorphous power networks' that act primarily in the interests of the capitalist class.[17] Some political institutions, such as bureaucracies, have been identified as major obstacles to change due to their possessing an inherent organisational bias to maintain the status quo, as discussed in Max Weber's *Economy and Society* (1925). Pluralists, however, are more likely to depict bureaucracies primarily as apolitical organisations that respond to and implement government policy.

'Transitology'

The wave of transitions from authoritarian rule since the 1970s in Latin America and other regions spawned a sub-discipline of 'transitology' that attempts to explain the changes. There are four main elements to the approach. First, structural factors are an inadequate means of explaining political change and more emphasis should be placed on the role of actors. Second, periods of transition are characterised by uncertainty, where decisions are being made in rapidly changing contexts and with insufficient information. Third, political actors are assumed to be rational and self-interested. Fourth, liberal democracy can only be achieved if the property rights of the wealthy are not challenged. A central text is this literature is the four-volume study, *Transitions from Authoritarian Rule* (1986), edited by Guillermo O'Donnell, Phillip Schmitter, and Laurence Whitehead. To some extent the transitologists have revived the emphasis on actors common in traditional history, while adopting some of the rational choice assumptions of economists.

Modernisation theory

A common perspective in political science since the 1950s is that stable liberal democracy emerges once a society has 'modernised' by passing through a linear progression of stages of development. This may be a gradual and cumulative process that includes meeting people's basic social and economic needs, providing literacy and other forms of education, ensuring a free media, having vibrant civic associationalism, developing a large middle class, urbanisation, and attaining sufficiently high average incomes. In 'Some Social Requisites of Democracy' (1959), an article that became a cornerstone of modernisation theory, Seymour Martin Lipset argued that democracy could not emerge unless a certain level of economic and social development had already been reached. Underlying such theories is the idea of empowerment, for instance that education enables voters to make informed choices and hold governments to account.

Modernisation theory contains a belief in the possibility of progress or human advancement, an idea developed by Enlightenment thinkers in the eighteenth century. The Enlightenment emerged in response to prevailing religious thinking that conceived of social relations and conditions as God-given and effectively static. Reason and science would help societies pass through various stages of development, from primitive to civilised. Holding an optimistic view of human nature, Enlightenment writers such as Voltaire envisaged a moral improvement of the human condition, in addition to greater material prosperity, social development, individual freedom and more accountable forms of political rule. One of the criticisms of the Enlightenment vision (that can also be applied to modernisation theory) is that it ignores the realities of the power of vested interests and élites in society who will prevent change, and that modern societies have exhibited degeneration as much as progress (as the Holocaust and the atomic bombing of Hiroshima and Nagasaki demonstrated). Such issues are discussed in one of the most famous critical analyses of the Enlightenment ideal of progress, *Dialectic of Enlightenment* (1944) by Theodore Adorno and Max Horkenheimer. The idea of linear historical progress is also criticised in the writings of post-modern philosopher of science Manuel de Landa who, drawing on ideas in complexity theory, conceives of a world of infinite variation.[18]

Sequences and demonstration effects

More complex than the linearity of modernisation theory is the idea that different sequences of change produce different outcomes or varying pathways. In *Problems of Democratic Transition and Consolidation* (1996), Juan Linz and Alfred Stepan specify around 20 different possible 'paths to democratic transition'.[19] The path a country takes depends on a range of factors and the sequence in which they emerge, such as prior regime type (for example authoritarian, totalitarian), civil-society autonomy, market autonomy, rule of law, and development of the state bureaucracy. The resulting forms of democracy will have diverse characteristics and face different problems of democratic consolidation. Such analyses of pathways of change often look back to Barrington Moore's classic study, *Social Origins of Dictatorship and Democracy: Lord and Peasant in the Making of the Modern World* (1966). He argued that there were three main routes to the modern world: first, the route of bourgeois revolution, where capitalism and parliamentary democracy combined following revolutionary upheaval (England, France, USA); second, conservative revolutions from above, and capitalism ending in fascism (Germany, Japan); and third, peasant revolutions leading to communism (Russia, China). His most cited conclusion is 'no bourgeois, no democracy': like Marx he argued that 'a vigorous and independent class of town dwellers has been an indispensable element in the growth of parliamentary democracy'.[20]

The study of sequences of change has received particular attention in quantitative political science through the use of 'path analysis models', which involve analysing networks and chains of causation. There are two primary models: 'recursive' path models, which do not include loops of causation; and 'non-recursive' path models, which do. The latter are difficult to analyse statistically, which is problematic because loops of causation are an extremely prevalent political phenomenon (for example approval of a party's policies can lead to identification with that party, but equally identification with the party can contribute to and reinforce approval for its policies). It is often unclear where to begin and end the causal analysis, and how to separate out various causal factors.[21]

A variation on the sequencing theme is the power of demonstration effects. This is the idea that developments in one place will act as a catalyst in another. One instance of this was the US fear of a 'domino effect' during the Cold War, the suggestion being that if one country, such as Viet Nam, fell to communism, then others would soon follow. The power of demonstration effects was evident in Eastern and Central Europe around 1989. Anti-government protest in one country encouraged a wave of similar protests across the region, leading to regime change in a number of countries. Demonstration effects are also apparent in social-movement theories about cycles of protest, and in the 'tipping point' argument (see the section on cross-disciplinary approaches below).

Consent and ideology

It has been common in political analysis to demonstrate how political and economic élites often use coercion to maintain their positions (for example military rule, police violence and intimidation, and extrajudicial death squads). But over recent decades there has been a growing focus on how they also employ more subtle, non-coercive means to generate consent in society and thereby legitimate their domination and existing institutions. For example, in the USA, scholars have shown how ideas such as 'America is the land of the free' and 'allegiance to the flag', which are taught to school children, help create an ideology that legitimises the governmental system and nation state.[22] In *The Age of Empire*

1875–1914 (1987), Eric Hobsbawm argues that ruling élites in Britain ensured their legitimacy and prevented democratic government from being overrun by the newly enfranchised masses through techniques such as the invention of nationalist traditions (in addition to strategies such as the provision of welfare to ameliorate social discontent).[23] Nationalist movements (which have been a major cause of social conflicts since the invention of nation-states in the eighteenth century), have also often used flags, dress, language, music, and the idolisation of heroes to generate consent among potential supporters. 'The nation' has come to be seen as an exemplary 'imagined community', a term popularised by Benedict Anderson.[24]

The idea of generating consent has been discussed through various concepts. Weber, for example, speaks of 'legitimation' and 'symbols of justification', Marx of 'dominant ideas', Durkheim of 'collective representations', Mosca of 'political formulae' or 'great suppositions', and Gramsci of 'hegemony'.[25] Although these various theories of consent generally concern how power is maintained, they imply that social change can take place by eroding the symbols, ideas, language, rituals, norms, and processes that help to generate consent for those in power.

Clientelism, patronage, and corruption

Political sociologists have studied how political systems can be pervaded by clientelism, patronage, and corruption. This might extend from straight bribery to more sophisticated systems where a political candidate promises a new road for a local community if the mayor can 'deliver' him the votes of the inhabitants. In the early twentieth century Weber identified this as a form of 'patriarchal domination' based on 'strictly personal loyalties'.[26] More recent studies include Judith Chubb's *Patronage, Power and Poverty in Southern Italy* (1982) and Frances Hagopian's *Traditional Politics and Regime Change in Brazil* (1996), which documents the informal and often illegal means by which large landowners have been able to maintain their economic and political privileges.[27] From this perspective, social change requires breaking down the traditional loyalties that underlie patronage systems, and the forms of bureaucratic organisation that promote them.

Inequality

Inequality has been identified as an important cause of political movements and social upheavals. The French Revolution, for instance, was partly a response to inequalities generated by centuries of authoritarian monarchical rule, evident in the cry for 'liberty, equality and fraternity'. But inequality means different things to different people. There are two main questions of discussion among scholars. First, inequality (or equality) of what? Some movements for change have sought equality of outcomes (for example income and assets, men and women sharing household roles) while others have pursued equality of opportunities (such as opportunity to access health and education systems, or equality before the law). Second, why is inequality a problem? On the one hand it can be conceived of as an intrinsic injustice or immorality. On the other, inequality can be a problem due to its consequences. For example, it can be more difficult for relatively poor people than for relatively wealthy people to afford good lawyers, to influence and gain access to the most important media corporations, or to incur the expenses of running for political office. That is, inequality of resources generated by market economies impedes the exercise of political and civil rights. This has encouraged some political scientists to stress a fundamental discord between capitalism and democracy.[28]

Sociology

In the mid twentieth century sociologists were primarily concerned not with how change happens, but how stability happens. The structural-functionalist theory of Talcott Parsons promoted a research culture focusing on how social systems functioned to maintain their unity and stability. Since then, sociologists have become more interested in change.

Social movements, civil society, and anarchic organisations

Social movements have been a major subject of sociological study since the 1960s, based on a realisation that collective organisation outside traditional party politics had a major impact on governments and the state (seen, for instance, in the civil-rights movement in the USA). Among the most important studies is Sidney Tarrow's *Power in Movement: Social Movements, Collective Action and Politics* (1994). In an analysis of social movements since the nineteenth century, he identifies four main factors that influence their impact: the structure of political opportunities (availability of allies, divisions among élites); the repertoires or forms of collective action (strikes, demonstrations, petitions, barricades, etc.); the organisation of networks of activists (formal, informal); and the ideological frameworks and symbols used by the movements. In addition, he stresses that social-movement activity is characterised by cycles of protest across social sectors, echoing the cyclical theories of change popular among classical historians. The literature on social action discusses how social activists have always faced decisions and dilemmas when attempting to bring about social change. For instance: should they focus on citizen organising, campaigning, popular education, advocacy, or direct action?; should they work within the system, facing the inherent dangers of co-optation, or work outside it?; should they aim for reformist or structural change?; what role should be given to leadership?; and should they pursue long-term or short-term objectives? Among the most important issues is whether to focus activity on the local, national, or global level, and understanding how these levels are related to each other.[29]

A significant intellectual development in the early 1980s was the revival of 'civil society' (an eighteenth-century idea) as an analytical category, partly inspired by anti-state movements such as 'Solidarity' in Poland. Civil society includes not only social movements, but also other organisations such as professional associations, independent media, and non-government organisations (NGOs), which can serve as intermediaries between the private and public spheres. The language of civil society has now been adopted by social analysts and activists in Latin America, Africa, and other regions. For civil-society theorists, the extent to which a society can change partly depends on the 'strength' of its civil society, which may refer to the degree of unity among various social organisations, the quality of leadership, the clarity of objectives, or other factors. A central text in this revival is John Keane's edited volume, *Civil Society and the State: New European Perspectives* (1988). In general, the explanations in the civil-society literature of how change happens overlap considerably with the explanations in the social-movements literature.

A third literature emerges from a libertarian socialist or anarchist tradition, concerning the idea that social change has been most effective when groups in society organise and operate outside the realms of the state and formal capitalist economic structures, rather than engage in reformist activities. Organisations are ideally non-hierarchical, local, voluntary, and operate on the basis of mutual aid. Examples include the long history of worker and consumer co-operatives, micro-credit schemes, voluntary organisations such as the Royal National Lifeboat Institution, intentional communities, the kibbutz movement, and the Human Scale Education movement. Discussions of this approach to social change include Colin Ward's *Anarchy in Action* (1973), and Ken Warpole's edited book *Richer Futures: Fashioning a New Politics* (1999).[30] The idea of 'affinity groups' – small groups who work together on direct action – can also be traced to anarchist thought.

Worldviews

There is a strong tradition of sociological analysis, apparent in the work of thinkers such as Karl Mannheim and Pierre Bourdieu, which investigates the 'worldviews' of social groups – their shared attitudes, unconscious thoughts and assumptions, and structures of belief.[31] Worldviews reflect our conditioned thinking, being a product of years of education, family influence, media propaganda, and social life. These worldviews, it is argued, provide a framework that shapes or guides our actions. A recent study of Guatemala's oligarchy or economic élite shows that a central aspect of their shared worldview is a deeply ingrained belief in the sanctity of private property. Their organised opposition to agrarian reform in the 1990s peace process was guided by, and absolutely consistent with, this deep belief in the private-property system. The possibility of supporting communal property ownership (advocated by many indigenous Mayan groups) was virtually 'unthinkable'.[32] The worldview limits the scope of possible actions. As an approach to how change happens, it shifts attention away from traditional thinking about 'cause and effect' or 'actors and structures' by placing social action in a deeper framework of meaning.

Scholars have identified three main ways that worldviews change. First, through new experiences; for example when many of those who volunteered to fight in twentieth-century wars became avowed pacifists because of their ordeals. Second, through new conversations; Daniel Goleman's work on 'emotional intelligence' describes 'empathy training programmes' in US prisons, in which inmates were directly exposed to their victims' perspectives and personal stories as a means of encouraging empathy and thereby reducing subsequent offences.[33] Third, through long-term changes in education systems; the causes and effects of climate change, for example, are now taught as part of the national curriculum in English schools. Discussions of how worldviews change also appear in the history of science (see the section below on technology and science).

Power

The modern study of power is rooted in the writings of Machiavelli and Hobbes, and has undergone a series of theoretical transformations in sociology, politics, and other disciplines. It is common to conceive of power as an entity that can be used by actors or institutions to instigate or prevent change. For instance, the military power of the state might be used to crush political opposition and uphold dictatorship.

Instead of conceiving of power as an entity that lies within institutions and that can be 'seized' or 'wielded', some analysts see power in relational terms, as a network or flow between institutions or individuals. This approach was pioneered by Michel Foucault. In *Discipline and Punish: The Birth of the Prison* (1975), he traces the growth of systems of social control in the west, arguing that since the eighteenth century there has been a shift from coercion to 'discipline' in organisations such as prisons, the police, and schools, through mechanisms including the use of timetables, surveillance, and administration. Here power is 'a technique which achieves its strategic effects through its disciplinary character'.[34]

Power is sometimes understood to have different 'dimensions'. A first dimension is that power involves *A* getting *B* to do something they would not otherwise do. A second dimension concerns non-observable power, for instance: *A* prevents issue *X* of relevance to *B* from reaching the agenda; or *B* doesn't place issue *X* on the agenda for fear of being punished by *A* for doing so. A third dimension is that *B* does not desire to have issue *X* on the agenda because *A* has influenced *B*'s desires such that *X* is 'unthinkable'. That is, *A* is able to manipulate *B*'s preferences or 'real interests'.[35] Each dimension of power has implications for how change happens. A first-dimension strategy might involve the use of force to bring about change. A third-dimension strategy might require the use of propaganda and education systems to reshape people's desires or worldviews.

Culture

Sociologists have a long history of interest in culture as a source of change. A famous study is Weber's *The Protestant Ethic and the Spirit of Capitalism* (1905), in which he investigated the conditions that made possible the development of capitalist civilisation. The spread of Calvinism, he argued, encouraged a new attitude towards the pursuit of wealth in post-Reformation Europe, influencing people to work in the secular world, develop their own enterprises, engage in trade, and accumulate wealth for investment. In the 1960s and 1970s, liberation theology was identified as a major cultural-religious force for social change in regions such as Latin America.

The role of culture in social change has re-emerged as a popular topic in the last decade, particularly due to the growth of fundamentalist Islamic and evangelical Christian movements. Samuel Huntington's *The Clash of Civilizations and the Remaking of the World Order* (1996) argues that post-Cold War conflict will increasingly occur along cultural or civilisational lines (e.g. Western, Islamic, Sinic, Hindu). Culture, not the state, will become the locus of war. The thesis has been criticised for helping to legitimise US foreign-policy aggression and failing to recognise the heterogeneity of the cultures analysed. Since the 1990s, studies of social trust and levels of happiness within and between countries have also revived cultural explanations of how change happens. An example is Robert Putnam's *Making Democracy Work: Civic Traditions in Modern Italy* (1993).

Social anthropology

Individual experience

A major development in the social sciences in the past 30 years has been the increasing legitimacy of subjective experience as an area of academic inquiry. Social anthropologists – and sociologists and oral historians – have become interested in how individuals experience their own lives and perceive the world. In a change linked to the development of 'history from below', the voices of ordinary people now take their place alongside the speeches of presidents. A pioneering book was Henry Mayhew's *London Labour and the London Poor* (1851). A classic example of the genre is Studs Terkel's *Working: People talk about what they do all day and how they feel about what they do* (1975), based on interviews with scores of workers from across the US social spectrum. In the developing world, an early and influential anthropological work was *The Children of Sanchez: Autobiography of a Mexican Family* (1961) by Oscar Lewis, about life in the slums of Mexico City.

The implications for understanding social change are profound. Instead of gauging the success of change by how much GDP per capita has grown, what new laws are in place, how often people vote in national elections, how long they live, and so on, the questions are now about whether individuals perceive any fundamental changes in their own lives. A related social-policy outcome is that it is now more common to ask people what kind of changes they want (though surveys, for example), rather than imposing them from the outside.

The analysis of how change happens is also altered. First, by focusing on people's personal stories and life choices, more emphasis is placed on the role of individual actors in explaining change. Second, it provides new perspectives on individuals' motivation to be involved in social action. Instead of assuming that voters or union activists are rational, self-interested, or class stooges, they are now revealed with their individual histories, contradictions, varying beliefs and values, desire for status and respect, and emotions. Third, it highlights the importance of how individuals (and societies) remember the past. For example, public acts of remembering can be crucial to processes of national reconciliation following social conflict, as witnessed in South Africa's Truth and Reconciliation Commission.[36] The consequences of historical amnesia were recognised by the philosopher George Santayana who wrote, 'Those who cannot remember the past are condemned to repeat it'.

Thick description

Social anthropologists are interested in why social processes occur although they tend not to rely on the mechanistic causal conceptions of change that dominate in other social sciences. The approach of 'thick description', pioneered by Clifford Geertz in his essay

'Deep Play: Notes on the Balinese Cockfight' (1973), involves the microscopic analysis of a specific context in a way that is highly participatory (for the researcher), usually qualitative, sensitive to circumstance, and that attempts to interpret meanings instead of discover causal laws. Such detailed analyses of particular contexts can help ground existing structural explanations of social change, show how various causal factors interact with each other, and provide greater understanding about the importance of individual actors.

Families and kinship systems

The anthropological interest in family and kinship networks adds significantly to an understanding of how change happens in societies, and the obstacles that prevent change. In *Guatemala: linaje y racismo* (1992), Marta Casaus focuses on Guatemala's 22 most important oligarchic 'family networks', which she believes operate to ensure oligarchic domination. Intermarriage within family networks unites the oligarchy, preventing splits between rural and urban business; families reproduce the dominant ideology – particularly racism – which provides oligarchic cohesion; and family networks help the élite secure state positions, permitting them to exercise economic and political influence.[37] It is not possible to explain, for example, why redistributive and expropriative land reform has not taken place in Guatemala, without understanding the pervasive influence and operation of these family networks. This kind of anthropological analysis is also common among political sociologists interested in the study of patronage systems and corruption.

Psychology

Nature and nurture

Most approaches to how change happens contain assumptions about human nature. Mainstream economic theories, for example, assume that individuals act in their own rational self-interest (see below). More than in any other discipline, psychologists have undertaken empirical research to understand the nature of human nature. Some believe that humans are innately selfish and aggressive. A more convincing literature argues that caring, compassion, and generosity are just as natural as selfishness and aggression. That is, the potential for empathy among human beings has been understated. A comprehensive analysis on the issue is Alfie Kohn's *The Brighter Side of Human Nature: Altruism and Empathy in Everyday Life* (1990). He cites a famous study by the US military of their soldiers in the Second World War, which showed that in the course of any single military engagement, over three-quarters of soldiers would not fire their weapon at all. That is, there was a marked reluctance to kill.[38] For the US military, making change happen (ensuring that, in the future, their soldiers were willing to fire their guns more often) required new training programmes that dehumanised 'the enemy'.

Views concerning the importance of nature versus nurture as determinants of human behaviour have passed through different phases. During the 1950s and 1960s it was common to believe that human actions were strongly influenced by social and cultural context. In the 1970s, the increased understanding of genetics triggered a swing towards the belief that our genetic make-up was a more important explanation of behaviour. In the past decade the pendulum has swung back towards a more mixed position, which emphasises the subtle interlinks between environmental and genetic factors in influencing how people behave. The central debates are discussed in Steven Pinker's article 'Why nature and nurture won't go away' (2004).

An implication of this debate is that attempting to bring about change through alterations in the social environment will have greater impact on behaviour that is shown to be strongly influenced by nurture, rather than that which is largely determined by nature.

Self-understanding and behaviourism

The general orientation of early twentieth-century psychology was towards thinking about the past experiences of individuals, rather than thinking about the future. Explanations for human actions and emotional states were frequently sought in the experiences of early childhood, most famously in the writings of Sigmund Freud, who believed that they were the source of many types of pathological conduct among adults. Freud also emphasised the unconscious motives behind human behaviour, as did Carl Jung.[39] How does change happen? That is, how does the individual deal successfully with pathological conduct? One, through the help of a professional analyst. Two, through developing a better understanding of their own pasts and the meanings of their dreams. Change comes from looking inwards at the self.

This approach is echoed in Buddhist thought concerned with the importance of self-awareness. In order to achieve worldly peace, writes the Buddhist monk Thich Nhat Hanh, we must begin with ourselves by 'being peace'. In contrast to Western psychology, this Buddhist self-awareness requires a focus on being in the present rather than an investigation of the past, or imaginings of the future. It also involves learning to empathise with the circumstances of others.[40]

Behavioural psychology, which became increasingly popular in the late twentieth century, places less emphasis on internal mental states than Freudian or Jungian psychology and instead suggests that individual behaviour can be changed through methods such as positive reinforcement, reward and punishment, and appeals to self-interest. As such, it also places limited importance on the role of worldviews and mindsets in shaping behaviour. Behavioural methods of change have been adopted in the fields of management (for example in change management and organisational leadership – see below) and personal coaching, where they have been combined with other psychological approaches, such as cognitivism, systems theory, and humanistic psychology (based on the work of Carl Rogers, for example).

Social psychology

Social psychology provides further insights into how change happens. Some of the most important work has been on the psychology of fear, and how fear has been manipulated for political purposes. An example is that many critics of the current US administration have argued that the government has, since 2001, encouraged a culture of fear of the threat of terrorism, which has made it easier to introduce legislation that erodes civil liberties.[41]

Another significant area of research with relevance for social change concerns cultures of denial. In *States of Denial: Knowing about Atrocities and Suffering* (2001), Stanley Cohen investigates the psychological basis of how we can know about human-rights abuses or poverty in many parts of the world yet remain indifferent or deny that we have any moral responsibility to act. He also analyses how it is possible to overcome mass phenomena such as 'passive bystanders' and 'compassion fatigue' so that publics and governments take action to prevent suffering and cruelty. Cohen points out that giving people more information won't help, and argues in favour of four strategies to overcome cultures of denial: education and prevention (for example education programmes about the bystander phenomenon); legal compulsion (for example making it a legal duty to assist somebody whose life is in danger); appeal (positive appeals to people's caring nature rather than using shame or guilt); and channelled acknowledgement (fundraising where donors don't have to make major investments of thought, time, or energy, such as fundraising credit cards).[42] Understanding the psychology of denial is also becoming increasingly important in environmental campaigning which attempts to tackle individual and social denial about the effects of climate change.

Economics

Economics was invented in the late nineteenth century as a derivative of political economy. Political economists such as Adam Smith frequently emphasised historical factors and precedents when explaining how economic change happens. This approach was inherited by early twentieth-century economic thinkers such as John Maynard Keynes. Yet by the end of the twentieth century, economists had largely abandoned history in their analysis of how change happens. Instead they created theoretical and applied models about human behaviour and how markets function. Mainstream neo-liberal economics had become isolated from social reality. This would not have surprised Karl Polanyi, whose influential book *The Great Transformation: The Political and Economic Origins of Our Time* (1944), argued that the assumptions of free-market economics (such as the idea that markets are 'self-regulating') had weak historical underpinnings.

Rational self-interest and collective action

Orthodox economics assumes that individuals in society are rational and self-interested decision makers (propounded in rational choice theory). Economists of this persuasion posit that, if faced with a choice between two identical products, you will buy the cheaper one. Sociologists and social anthropologists would not make this assumption, believing that individuals often base their decisions on habit, emotion, or other factors (for Max Weber 'instrumental rational action' was only one of four types of social action). From the perspective of most economic theory, individual behaviour will change in accordance with rational self-interest. Amartya Sen famously described rational economic man as 'close to being a social moron'.[43]

A related issue in economics is how people make decisions when their interests are in conflict, or if there is uncertainty about how other people will act. The most rational, self-interested decision in these circumstances may be to co-operate with other people. Such issues are at the core of game theory and collective-action problems, including the prisoners' dilemma problem. A central text on these matters is Mancur Olson's *The Logic of Collective Action* (1971).

The assumptions of rational self-interested actors and game theory have had considerable influence in other disciplines, such as the study of voting behaviour by political scientists and international relations. This is a significant development in intellectual history as it shifts discussion of issues such as how change happens away from empirical analysis to a more abstract, theoretical level.

The invisible hand

The central theory of modern capitalist economics is that resources are most effectively distributed in a free market, operating with minimal external regulation. If buyers and sellers meet in the marketplace, under conditions of perfect information, then a stable equilibrium is reached where demand equals supply. Despite the intentions of buyers and sellers to act in their own self-interest, goods and services are distributed in the best interests of society by an 'invisible hand', first described by Adam Smith in *The Theory of Moral Sentiments* (1759). So how does change happen? First, when there are changes in the preferences of individual consumers. Second, when there are changes in the stocks and supplies of factors of production – land, labour, capital, enterprise, and other economic resources – in addition to major advances in technology. Endogenous growth theory puts a particular emphasis on technological change and innovation within the economic system as a cause of long-term growth. Joseph Schumpeter's notion of 'creative destruction' provides a further framework of competition and innovation. The theory of comparative advantage helps explain how specialisation develops among different producers, hence promoting trade.

Achieving change by using markets is discussed below in Part 3, along with several other strategies of economic and social development.

Heterodox economics

By the end of the 1980s there was broad agreement among North American economists and policy technocrats in the World Bank and International Monetary Fund (IMF) that economic growth required three main reforms: stabilisation, liberalisation, and privatisation. This package, which became known as the 'Washington Consensus', placed particular emphasis on trade liberalisation and rolling back the state. However, by the late 1990s it became clear that such policies had provided disappointing results, particularly in developing countries. Harvard economist Dani Rodrik is at the forefront of those who highlight the fact that some of the most successful growth performers have followed unconventional heterodox policies and 'have marched to the beat of their own drummers'.[44] China, for example, grafted a market system onto a planned system (rather than totally abandoning the latter), downplayed private-property rights (relying instead on township-and-village enterprises owned by local governments), and opened up to the world in a partial way (by complementing a highly protectionist trade regime with special economic zones). Viet Nam, India, Japan, Korea, and Taiwan have also experienced significant growth without following the orthodox free-market ideal.

As a means of bringing about change in terms of economic growth, Rodrik advocates policy diversity and experimentation that suit specific economies as opposed to 'one-size-fits-all' policy blueprints. He also stresses that reform objectives should focus on identifying the most significant bottleneck in an economy (such as inadequate levels of private investment and entrepreneurship, for example) and working to alleviate that bottleneck. Additionally, he argues that there are four 'first-order' principles of economic policy that all successful economies have adhered to: maintaining macro-economic stability; integrating into the world economy; protecting property rights and contract enforcement; and ensuring social cohesion, solidarity, and political stability.[45]

Feminist economics

Feminist economists criticise their more orthodox colleagues for confining themselves to studying the 'paid economy' of markets and prices. A large amount of goods and services produced – such as agricultural production, meals, housing, clothing, health care – happens outside the monetised economy. Similarly, human capital – a critical 'asset' for economies – is produced mostly through unpaid, caring labour. These goods and services are produced predominantly by women. The fact that women and men do different kinds of work springs from a combination of social norms and institutions, and natural difference (for example women give birth and breast-feed). Feminist economists highlight the different value attributed by society to the work of women and men, and argue that this is both an outcome and a driver of systematic bias against women in society. This bias is transmitted through a variety of institutions, such as the family, markets (labour, finance), and the state, and can result in gender differences in education, wages, use of technology and access to credit, to name only a few. The originality of feminist economics with respect to how change happens lies in arguing that achieving gender equality and sustainable human development requires recognising the economic value of the unpaid economy and developing public policy on the basis of this recognition.[46]

Corporate power

The main criticism of the idea of the invisible hand and the self-regulating market is that it is a theory. The reality is that the so-called 'free' market contains and generates market failures and distortions such as monopoly, oligopoly, corruption, and illegal activities such as non-compliance with labour laws. This has spawned more empirically-based, alternative literatures on how economies function.

An example is the study of corporate and business power, with one of the most influential early studies being Michael Josephson's *The Robber Barons* (1934), about nineteenth-century US titans such as J. P. Morgan and John D. Rockefeller. This literature highlights four main characteristics of corporations. First, that their overriding priority is to maximise profits and shareholder value. Other policies or strategies, such as pursuing corporate social responsibility and environmental programmes, will remain secondary unless they contribute to profit maximisation. Second, that they enjoy political privileges: governments are partly beholden to corporations due to their reliance on large firms for party political funding and to maintain economic stability. This helps explain why they receive large government subsidies and other benefits.[47] Third, that they enjoy legal advantages. In the USA, many of these advantages developed in the late nineteenth century, for example the precedent that corporations were 'persons' and that their money was properly protected by the due process clause of the Fourteenth Amendment (which had actually been passed to protect Negro rights).[48] Fourth, that they will frequently resort to corrupt practices such as bribery and false accounting to maintain profits and protect market share, as the case of Enron illustrates. All these issues are addressed in Joel Bakan's *The Corporation* (2004), which focuses on the legal basis of contemporary corporate domination. The implications for how change happens are that major corporations such as General Electric or Exxon Mobil are best seen not as agents of change but as obstacles to it. They are like the medieval Christian church: among the most privileged and conservative forces in society, with the power to maintain the status quo.

In contrast, there is a growing literature on how businesses can be a socially benign force for social change. Such analyses argue that under consumer pressure or legal compulsion, corporations can act in the public good. Social entrepreneurship, and employee activism and share ownership, also contribute to a context in which business is not simply about making profits. These ideas are reflected in the concept of corporate social responsibility (see discussion below).

Management and organisational studies

Learning organisations

How do organisations, particularly businesses, bring about change in their own activities and adapt to changes in the marketplace? These are questions at the centre of management and organisational studies. An exemplary analysis is Peter Senge's *The Fifth Discipline: The Art and Practice of the Learning Organisation* (1992), which was responsible for popularising the idea of the 'learning organisation'. He argues that in situations of rapid change only those organisations that are flexible, adaptive, and productive will excel, and in order to do so they need to become 'learning organisations' that discover how to tap people's commitment and capacity to learn. While he believes that all people have the capacity to learn, he argues that the structures in which they function are typically not conducive to reflection and engagement. A learning organisation must master five basic disciplines: 'systems thinking' involves having a long-term view of the organisation and integrating the other four disciplines; 'personal mastery' requires individuals being open to learning and having a personal vision of the organisation and their place in it; 'mental models' refers to the need to understand our ingrained assumptions and generalisations that shape our actions, similar to the sociological idea of worldviews; 'building shared vision' must be a primary objective of organisational leaders; and 'team learning' builds on personal mastery and shared vision. Overall, this approach suggests that organisations can bring about change and adapt to it most effectively when they develop both a long-term vision and learn to see themselves as an organic and flexible whole. Senge's theory has been criticised for operating at the level of organisational interests and failing to have any moral or political framework.[49]

More recent work by Senge and other learning theorists on systems change and sustainability advocates change as emerging from collaboration across a number of systems and sectors. Innovation and change come from stepping outside institutional or sectoral boundaries, and understanding the wider 'ecosystem' in which change happens.[50]

Stages of change

Another classic model in change management and organisational studies, originally based on research on the processes of grieving by Elisabeth Kubler-Ross (discussed in her book *On Death and Dying*, 1969), is that individuals pass through a number of stages when adjusting to challenging situations, such as apprehension, denial, anger, resentment, depression, cognitive dissonance, compliance, acceptance, and internalisation. Making organisational change happen requires being aware that personnel may need to pass through such stages to fully integrate the change into their working practices and lives. There is also emphasis in the literature on the need for staff to be actively involved in change processes at all levels, and supported through them.[51] Such models have been criticised for being empirically innaccurate and – like modernisation theory – excessively linear. They resemble political-science ideas concerning the importance of analysing sequences of change.

Leadership

Traditional approaches to leadership from within the management and organisational studies field have a behavioural emphasis, advising leaders to use standard rewards like pay and promotions to encourage their workers and bring about change. Others suggest that leaders should not be authoritarian commanders but instead act as 'stewards' or 'teachers', who are willing to sacrifice their personal self-interest for the good of the organisation as a whole. Another recent trend is to stress that the most effective organisational leaders are charismatic and inspiring, and appeal to the emotions and values of their workers or members.[52] The very idea of 'leadership' echoes top-down theories of history although the stress on developing sensitivity to the individual experience of workers, rather than focusing solely on structural change, illustrates an openness to the insights of anthropology and sociology in the management and organisational studies literature.

International relations and globalisation

Realism

During the Cold War, the study of how change happens in international relations was limited to two primary, rather simplistic, theories: realism and idealism. Realists argued that the international system is effectively a Hobbesian state of war of all against all, in which states operate in their own best interests. The history of US foreign policy, such as the unilateral invasion of countries such as Panama, Haiti, and Granada, in addition to the invasions of Iraq and Afghanistan, gives credence to the realist approach. It asserts that realignments of the international system generally take place when there is a shift in the international balance of power, for instance through the emergence of powerful new states (such as China today). Realism implies that the most effective way to change the system is to appeal to, or alter, the national interests of states.

Idealism

The contrasting idealist tradition is that, taken together, states constitute a potential community of mankind, in which international co-operation that goes beyond national self-interest is possible. This is evident, for example, in the establishment of the United Nations (UN) and various international covenants on human rights. In this scenario, international agreements, consensus, and compromise can be the basis of global change (enacted, for instance, through dialogue processes to end armed conflicts). Similarly, as Hedley Bull argued in *The Anarchical Society: A Study of Order in World Politics* (1977), international order in a world of sovereign nation states has been ensured not only by mechanisms such as balance of power, but by international law, diplomacy, and the conventions of war. Idealist theories in international relations are closely related to pluralist theories in political science, and are based on a more altruistic conception of human nature than the Hobbesian perspective that underlies realism.

Globalisation

Various theories of globalisation, which have emerged since the end of the Cold War, suggest that nation states are no longer sovereign actors in the international system. They have become increasingly subject to factors such as shifts in international capital markets and commodity prices, the influence of multinational corporations, the rulings of international legal tribunals, and the rules and regulations of transnational bodies such as the World Trade Organisation (WTO), the World Bank, and the IMF. The global anti-capitalist movement's targeting of such international organisations in their campaigns for social and economic justice is evidence that the locus of change is shifting away from nation states. Many globalisation theories have their roots in older approaches to the international system such as world systems theory and dependency theory.

These theories are discussed and elaborated in Paul Viotti and Mark Kauppi's *International Relations Theory: Realism, Pluralism, Globalism* (1993), and are critiqued in Fred Halliday's *Rethinking International Relations* (1994).

Geography

Environment and society

Several sub-fields of geography, notably human geography and environmental geography, focus on how people shape their environment and how environments shape individual lives and human societies. These sub-fields have received a boost in popularity in recent years through the publication of Jared Diamond's *Guns, Germs and Steel: A Short History of Everybody for the Last 13,000 Years* (1998), which attempts to explain broad global variations in human development, such as why Europe became wealthy and powerful but Africa did not. His analysis draws primarily on geography, but also genetics, molecular biology, behavioural ecology, epidemiology, the history of technology and political organisation, linguistics, and archaeology. He provides four main explanations for regional variations in human development. First, continental differences in the wild animal and plant species available as starting materials for domestication, which shaped the ability of different peoples to develop food production and accumulate food surpluses. Second, differential rates of diffusion and migration of technology, crops, livestock, and people within continents. For instance, rugged terrain prevented political and linguistic unification in some regions. Third, factors affecting diffusion between continents: Australian Aborigines, for example, were geographically isolated from the technological advances of Eurasia. Fourth, continents with larger areas and populations advanced because they had more potential innovators and more pressure to innovate because of greater competition among their various societies.[53] In sum, change is explained by a range of environmental differences between continents, and not by racial differences between peoples.

The importance of geography in influencing the shape of political, social, and economic development is also evident in the work of eighteenth-century thinkers such as Montesquieu and in the writings of economist Jeffrey Sachs (who makes direct reference to *Guns, Germs and Steel*).[54]

Urban geography

Urban geographers have confronted the problems caused by mass urbanisation in the Western world since the eighteenth century, and in the developing world from the twentieth. Urbanisation has brought about some of the most significant changes in human societies, for instance: acute poverty produced by capitalist industrialisation, as discussed in David Harvey's *Social Justice and the City* (1973); the breakdown of communal organisation and living, documented in Murray Bookchin's *From Urbanization* to Cities (1995); disease epidemics such as cholera, discussed in David Weatherall's *Science and the Quiet Art* (1995); new forms of crime, violence, and surveillance, analysed in Mike Davis's *City of Quartz: Excavating the Future in Los Angeles* (1992); and a host of housing, educational, and other problems faced by specific groups such as children, brilliantly explored in Colin Ward's *The Child in the City* (1979). Geographers have also been sensitive to demographic change, for instance the way that population growth in many developing countries has put pressure on urban settlements and services, or how the HIV and AIDS pandemic has decimated particular communities.

The social changes investigated by urban geographers have contributed to efforts to redesign cities, giving urban planning an important status as a force for change. A significant instance of the impact of town planning was the establishment in post-Second World War Britain of 'garden cities', based on a model invented by Ebenezer Howard in the late nineteenth century. Located on the periphery of existing urban settlements, they were designed to provide green spaces, and improve housing and sanitation for poor urban workers. These and other attempts at urban redesign appear in Lewis Mumford's classic *The Culture of Cities* (1938). In developing countries, in contrast, the lack of affordable housing has often led to the creation of shanty towns, where members of poor communities have taken social organisation and change into their own hands. The realities of life in the shanty towns of Brazil are discussed in Teresa Caldeira's *City of Walls: Crime, Segregation and Citizenship in São Paulo* (2000).

Cultural geography

Cultural geographers are interested in how geographic space is defined or 'imagined', that is, how individuals and social groups think about ideas such as 'the city' or 'the nation', and the consequences this has for social change (see the discussion on consent and ideology above). Over the past two decades in Guatemala, for example, indigenous people have increasingly self-identified as 'Mayans', as opposed to describing themselves as being members of one of around two dozen language groups (for example Ixil) with close ties to specific geographical locations. This transformation of identity has had an impact on social change through contributing to the development of a pan-Mayan political movement campaigning for cultural and economic rights in a highly racist society.[55]

Geographers have been at the forefront of exploring changes in people's lives brought about by the Internet and new forms of communication, evident in Manuel Castells' trilogy, *The Information Age* (1996–1998). He argues that the infrastructure of the Internet has been shaped by the conflicting agendas of the state (military, academia), social movements (hackers, social activists), and business interests. Castells believes that modern societies are increasingly structured around the bipolar opposition of the 'Net' and the 'Self', where the Net refers to the networked forms of organisation that are replacing hierarchies as the dominant form of social organisation, and the Self concerns the multiple identities of individuals shaped by contexts of rapid change.

Legal studies

Laws change through a variety of mechanisms, such as precedent, statutory interpretation, legislation, and constitutional amendment. But laws also impact on broader aspects of change. 'The structure of every legal order', wrote Max Weber in *Economy and Society* (1925), 'directly influences the distribution of power, economic or otherwise, within its respective community'.[56] Law acts as an intermediary between individuals (e.g. family law), between companies (e.g. corporate law), between states (e.g. international law), and between individuals and institutions (e.g. labour law). So how do legal-studies scholars think about the relationship between law and social change?

Individual and group rights

One perspective is the idea that law can help respect, protect, and fulfil individual human rights. In general, legal systems (particularly in the West) have been far better at serving this function with respect to civil and political rights than with respect to social and economic rights. In the past three decades there has been a growing belief that legal systems at both the national and international level should and can respect, protect, and fulfil group rights, particularly those of indigenous people. A major issue is whether indigenous people are able to use legal systems to reclaim traditional lands that they may have lost during colonial conquests. A text on these debates is Will Kymlicka's edited collection, *The Rights of Minority Cultures* (1995).

There is evidence that legal systems are able to bring about significant change, especially for previously marginalised sectors of society. Civil-rights legislation in the USA in the 1960s ended racist practices such as segregation. In Australia in the 1990s, advances were made in establishing Aboriginal land rights through various favourable 'native title' legal decisions.

A significant problem for this optimistic view of law is that many laws exist on paper but are not upheld in practice. International human-rights law has been notoriously difficult to enforce. Similarly, in many developing countries it is standard practice for firms to ignore national labour laws with impunity. Disabilities groups in the UK have struggled for decades to have their legal rights in the workplace respected in practice. Women likewise continue to experience discrimination at work despite equal-opportunity laws.

Law as privilege, coercion, and social control

A critical approach argues that law primarily functions to maintain the status quo, rather than to secure individual or group rights. In his essay 'Law and Authority' (1927), the nineteenth-century anarchist Peter Kropotkin wrote that legal systems operated to protect the private property of the wealthy, and to protect the privileges and power of the state. This model suggests that legal systems are an ineffective means of achieving change. What is the evidence?

Almost every constitution in every country protects and privileges the institution of private property, which forms the basis of all capitalist economies.[57] Similarly, legal systems in countries such as the USA have systematically favoured large corporations, as Joel Bakan argues in *The Corporation* (2004). Governments have long histories of using law as a mechanism of coercion, for instance through banning trade-union activities in certain industries. Latin American military dictators in the 1960s and 1970s manipulated laws to ensure that their rule was 'legal'. Moreover, due to judicial corruption, underfunding, and other factors, legal systems in Latin America have largely failed to bring former dictators to account for their role in human-rights violations. Shari'a law serves to discriminate against women in areas such as inheritance, marriage, and divorce.[58] Many of these problems emerge from the fact that laws need to be interpreted and the interpreters (for example judges, Afghan mullahs) bring their own assumptions and prejudices into their rulings.

Legal systems have, however, sometimes been used to bring powerful actors and institutions to account for their actions, which has happened in recent years with tobacco companies in the USA. Such actions have been most effective where there is a strong legal infrastructure, for instance an absence of corruption, public scrutiny of the legal system, and co-ordination between different government institutions (such as the police and the judiciary).

The positive and negative role that law has played in shaping the lives of women, indigenous people, children, and other groups in society, is discussed in texts such as *Before the Law: An Introduction to the Legal Process* (1998) by Bonsignore *et al.*

Technology and science

The impact of new technologies

New technologies and scientific invention have been among the most important sources of change in human history. Inventions such as bronze, the stirrup, the printing press, the spinning jenny, electricity, penicillin, contraception, and the Internet have transformed areas such as warfare, economic development, human health, gender relations, and global communication. In *The Greatest Benefit to Mankind: A Medical History of Humanity from Antiquity to the Present* (1997), Roy Porter cites the global eradication of smallpox as one of the great triumphs of medical science. This began with the invention of inoculation methods in eighteenth-century Europe, when in bad years smallpox was responsible for around one-tenth of all deaths. It ended with a major World Health Organisation vaccination programme in the 1960s and 1970s. This was the first time a disease had been entirely eliminated by human intervention.[59] The general effects of new technologies on social change are discussed in Daniel Boorstin's *The Discoverers: A History of Man's Search to Know his World and Himself* (1985).

Technological innovation is considered to have several sources. First, it can be a product of demand, supply, and competition. For instance, in the eighteenth century, the British government offered a prize for developing an instrument to provide the precise determination of a ship's longitude, resulting in a new invention by the clock-maker John Harrison. Alternatively, technological innovation can be a result of human creativity (see below). Another debate about technological change concerns the way it diffuses through society. In *Diffusion of Innovations* (1962), Everett Rogers argued that innovations would spread in an 'S-curve', with a small group of 'early adopters' selecting the technology first, followed by the majority, until a technology or innovation had become common. 'Innovators', he argued, tended to be educated and risk-takers, whereas 'the majority' were characterised as being sceptical, traditional, and having lower socio-economic status.

Sources of creativity

If new technologies are a product of human creativity, how does that creativity happen? Some of the leading theories of creativity highlight the following sources: lateral thinking; analogical reasoning to make connections between different spheres of knowledge; unveiling assumptions and underlying metaphors; experimental processes; individual genius; collaboration between individuals; psychoticism; neural structure; and chance. Arthur Koestler's *The Act of Creation* (1964) argues that creativity arises due to the intersection of two different frames of reference. Edward De Bono's *Lateral Thinking* (1970) is among the best-known textbooks on creative thinking.

Paradigm shifts

A significant theory of how scientific change happens appears in Thomas Kuhn's *The Structure of Scientific Revolutions* (1962). He argued that scientists operate within the assumptions of the dominant paradigm of their time (for example the assumptions of Newtonian physics or Einstein's theory of relativity). Scientific advancement has not been a gradual process of accumulating knowledge. Rather, there have been occasional 'paradigm shifts' in which the shared worldview or framework for understanding in specific scientific communities is replaced by a new paradigm. He suggested that while the transformation of scientists' worldviews can be likened to 'switches in visual gestalt', in practice the shift generally occurs slowly as established scientists may be reluctant to adjust and because it takes time to reorient the educational system to teach students to see the new gestalt.[60] The parallels with sociological theories about worldviews are clear.

Philosophy

Dialectical reasoning

The most important theory of change in the history of philosophy is dialectic, a form of logical reasoning. This is the view that a collision between two contradictory ideas can be synthesised to produce a new idea which is a 'higher truth'. The idea of dialectic is evident in Socratic method and was theorised by Hegel. It was then adopted and transformed by Marx, who held that the process of history is a dialectical development in which humankind progresses through the clash of contradictory social systems. Bertrand Russell believed that the dialectical method is most appropriate when discussing concepts and cannot be used to help discover new facts.[61]

Falsification

Karl Popper was one of the most vociferous critics of the dialectical method. In his view, human knowledge advances through the investigation of empirically falsifiable hypotheses (for example the hypothesis that 'all swans are white', which can be falsified by the observation of one black swan). Kuhn's work on the structure of scientific revolutions found little evidence that science develops in the way described by Popper. Another critic of Popper was his student Paul Feyerabend who, in *Against Method* (1975), argued that the only universally valid methodological rule to advance knowledge was 'anything goes'. Hence he advocated, for example, the use of counterfactual hypotheses in scientific and other areas of research.

Multiple ways of knowing

In recent decades the idea of objective knowledge has been questioned in philosophy and other disciplines through the rise of discourse analysis and critical theory, often associated with thinkers such as Michel Foucault and Jacques Derrida. The emphasis of analysis is on texts, language, symbols, and meanings, and the idea that the meaning of an object is socially constructed. For instance, 'a forest might be an object of intrinsic natural beauty, an obstacle to the building of a motorway, or a unique ecosystem, depending on the horizon of classificatory rules and differences that confers meaning to it'.[62] Several other ideas are associated with this approach to knowledge, for example: that the models and theories on which we base our understanding are only partial representations of reality; that the validity of an idea in an organisation is connected to the relative power of the idea's proponents; and that ideas cannot be detached from the person holding those ideas. What are the implications for how change happens? First, when we undertake our own analyses of social change we should be aware of the assumptions and power relations underlying how we construct our approach. Second, we should be conscious of the way that language itself can shape social change; for instance that ideas such as 'law and order' or 'terrorist' can be manipulated by politicians to achieve their political objectives. In general, however, discourse analysis has been criticised for an excessive focus on interpreting texts and meanings, and being insufficiently oriented towards understanding social change.

Ecology

How do ecologists and evolutionary biologists think about how change happens? There are four primary approaches.

Natural selection and selfish genes

The first is that evolutionary change takes place through processes of natural selection and 'survival of the fittest'. At first this was thought to take place at the species level but it is now more common to think about such processes occurring at the genetic level, as popularised in Richard Dawkins' book, *The Selfish Gene* (1976), where he writes that 'all life evolves by the differential survival of replicating entities'. There is a strong corollary with economists' assumptions about self-interested actors, although Dawkins believes his theory (which remains controversial) can also explain altruistic behaviour.

Adherents of 'social Darwinism' in the late nineteenth and early twentieth centuries held that the biological idea of natural selection through competition could be extended to the analysis of societies. While some societies flourish, it claims, others are destined to die out due to the primitive and inferior characteristics of their people. This ideology formed the basis of theories of racial supremacy and eugenics, which were largely discredited by the middle of the twentieth century.

Mutual interdependence and symbiotic relationships

Second is the idea that ecosystems are characterised by mutual interdependence and symbiotic relationships. An example is mycorrhizal fungus in the soil that attaches itself to tree and plant roots. The fungus takes some goodness from the roots to survive, while at the same time helping draw in water and nutrients to the roots that the roots can't reach themselves. The roots and the fungus need each other.[63] Similarly, in his book *Biophilia: The human bond with other species* (1984), Edward O. Wilson describes the extraordinary interdependence and co-operation at work in ant colonies in the Brazilian Amazon.[64] In contrast, predation relationships (where one species relies on another as a food source) are examples of interdependence that do not entail symbiosis and co-operation. Altering one aspect of an ecosystem generally has far-reaching consequences for the survival of other parts of the ecosystem, and can result in the demise of whole species and a reduction in biodiversity. The general lesson of such interdependence is that change in one realm can have unintended consequences in another.

This emphasis on interdependence and co-operation is reflected in anarchist theories of social organisation and mutual aid. The idea of interdependence also has close parallels with the theory of the 'butterfly effect', an element of chaos theory. This is the notion that small variations in the initial condition of a dynamic system may create large variations in the long-term behaviour of the system.

Self-regulation

A third approach is that not only are life forms highly integrated and mutually interdependent, but that the earth as a whole should be considered a single, self-regulating organism. This idea is described in James Lovelock's *Gaia: A New Look at Life on Earth* (1979). Lovelock's theory suggests, for instance, that if one species becomes too dominant (e.g. human beings), over time various mechanisms (e.g. epidemics) may emerge and operate to reduce the population drastically, bringing the system as a whole to a sustainable and stable equilibrium, although one which may be far less favourable to human life.[65] This has some connections with the idea of a self-regulating market in economics, and with Thomas Malthus's theory in his *An Essay on the Principle of Population* (1798) that excessive population increases are naturally checked by occurrences such as famine and the spread of disease. The idea of self-regulation has been recently popularised through discussions of 'emergence theory', which concerns the way that biological, social, and technological systems (from ant colonies to the Internet) self-organise from the bottom up, as explored in Steven Johnson's *Emergence* (2002).

Climate change and unpredictability

Fourth are the approaches to change underlying studies of climate change. Like historians, climate-change experts are interested in how the world changed in the past, but there is a much greater acknowledgement that the world may change in unpredictable ways in the future. Some scientists believe that global temperatures will increase gradually over time. Others believe that once a specified level of increase has been reached (e.g. 2 degrees Celsius), this will trigger an acceleration and spiral of temperature increases and consequent ecological destruction. These various approaches are discussed in Bill McKibben's *The End of Nature* (1999). Important general lessons from this literature are that the past may not be a reliable guide to change in the future, and that how change happens may change over time.

Cross-disciplinary approaches to how change happens

The development of independent academic disciplines over the past century has resulted in isolation and overspecialisation.[66] Economists, for example, have learned very little from sociologists about human motivation, and generally maintain simplistic assumptions about human nature. Political scientists primarily focus on institutional processes, and rarely draw on the insights of social psychologists about the determinants of individual and group behaviour. Some disciplines have focused on quantitative research, and consider qualitative research to be lacking in rigour and objectivity. Others engage mainly with current, observable phenomena, and do not possess the long view encountered among historians. Experts in one discipline frequently find it impossible to understand the abstruse language or mathematical formulae in the journal articles of another. The lack of conversations between disciplines has limited our understanding of how change happens.

However, in the past two decades there has been a growth of cross-disciplinary research that attempts to draw on what has been learned across a range of scholarly traditions. Crossing the boundaries between disciplines has yielded some of the most significant and original approaches to how change happens. Here I would like to highlight two of them.

Tipping points

What causes rapid change in human societies? The best-known recent analysis is Malcolm Gladwell's *The Tipping Point: How Little Things Can Make a Big Difference* (2000), based on research in diverse fields such as social psychology, marketing, media studies, criminology, and epidemiology. Using a threshold model of collective behaviour familiar in the social sciences, he argues that some phenomena spread rapidly when they reach a 'tipping point' of social participation or popularity. One of his examples concerns Hush Puppies, a brand of shoes. Having become unpopular in the USA, the tipping point came in 1994 and 1995 when sales suddenly shot up. This wasn't through an advertising campaign. It was because a few kids in New York's East Village and Soho began wearing them, and the fad spread so that Hush Puppies became a cultural icon.

The important issue is how this rapid spreading takes place. Gladwell bases his argument on several ideas. First, that some people are better than others at making something spread, such as by having better social connections or more enthusiasm (The Law of the Few). Second, that there are specific ways to present or structure information to make it more memorable and effective (The Stickiness Factor). Third, that human behaviour can be changed through very small changes in people's immediate environment, for instance removing graffiti from walls in subway stations can cut crime (The Power of Context).[67]

Personal relationships and mutual understanding

In books such as *An Intimate History of Humanity* (1995) and *Conversation* (1998), historian Theodore Zeldin argues that the most important changes in human history have not occurred through the imposition or evolution of new political institutions, economic systems, or laws, but rather through individuals developing deeper understanding of the perspectives and experiences of others, and changing the way they treat one another on a personal level. For instance, western governments began introducing legislation to ensure greater equality between men and women over a century ago. Yet new laws have not eradicated discrimination against women in the workplace or domestic violence. The real changes, according to Zeldin, have come through men and women learning to talk with each other, and with men learning how to empathise with the experiences of women.[68]

For Zeldin, fundamental social change requires overcoming misunderstandings and ignorance about people from different cultures, occupations, genders, generations, and social backgrounds. A method of doing so is to create one-to-one conversations between strangers where they get beyond superficial talk and speak about their lives on a personal and emotional level. This would be a microcosmic, personal, and long-term form of social change.[69] A similar approach to change has been promoted through 'empathy training programmes' in prisons (see the section on sociology), 'immersion programmes' run by development agencies, and grassroots peacebuilding and reconciliation projects based on developing personal connections between participants. These initiatives suggest that society can change by creating and encouraging empathy.

Part 2: The rough guide to how change happens

The conclusion I draw from the above analysis is that there are no generally applicable models of how social change happens. Every context has its own history and its own particularities. While there are some broad patterns, for instance that liberal democratic government rarely emerges if there has not been a fundamental division between rural and urban economic élites at some point in the past, these are far from being iron laws. The past is not a definitive guide to the future.

The explanations given for how change happens are also strongly shaped by the disciplinary perspective that is taken. Each discipline contains different assumptions about human motivation and behaviour, and the role of institutions and worldviews. They also each employ a variety of research methods, and study a range of time periods, geographical regions and forms of change, which, unsurprisingly, yields different results.

There is no need, however, to feel utterly dazed and confused. The various approaches to how change happens described in Part 1 generally address at least one of four major questions (mentioned at the beginning of this paper) that occur across disciplines:

- Who or what was involved in the change? (e.g. individual actors or state institutions)
- What strategies were used to bring about the change? (e.g. reformism, mass mobilisation)
- What were the contexts that affected how the change happened? (e.g. urbanisation, power relationships)
- What was the process or pathway of change? (e.g. demonstration effects, cumulative progress)

I have used these questions to create a tool for thinking about how change happens, based on a thematic summary of the discussion above. It is in the form of a table called 'The rough guide to how change happens' (see below). To repeat, this does not provide a set of models of change. Rather, it encourages you to draw on diverse academic disciplines in explaining how a change has happened. It provides a list of possible ingredients, not a recipe, and it is up to you to decide how to combine them, and then weave them into a narrative.

The 'rough guide' can be used to analyse how past changes have taken place. This requires the following steps:

- Identify a change that you want to explain, such as: what explains the rise of crime and violence in Latin American cities over the past decade?; why has there been growth in Chinese investment in Africa?; what explains the increase in Fair Trade sales in Europe since the mid 1990s?
- Then go through each of the following questions in the table (in the left-hand column) in turn, asking yourself whether and how its corresponding themes and categories (in the right-hand column) are relevant.

Table 1: The rough guide to how change happens[70]

In order to understand how a particular change occurred, ask yourself the questions in the left-hand column, while considering the possibilities appearing in the right-hand column – all of which feature in explanations of change across academic disciplines.

ASK YOURSELF...	REMEMBER TO THINK ABOUT...
1. What is the change that you want to explain? What was the situation before the change? And what was the situation after it?	Before-and-after contrasts in: • Behaviour of, and relations between, individuals and/or groups • Policies and practices of institutions (state, private sector, civil-society organisations) • Social attitudes and beliefs • The state of the natural environment • The state of human well-being
2. Who or what was involved in the change? Identify all relevant actors who: • were changed • were active agents of change • facilitated the change • resisted the change	People, as: • Individuals • Social groups (such as women workers, indigenous people) Institutions of: • State (executive, military, judiciary, bureaucracy, political parties) • Society (development NGOs, religious organisations, unions, the media) • Economy (corporations, small and medium-sized enterprises, informal workers, unpaid care-givers) • Global governance (WTO, World Bank, UN)
3. What strategies were used to bring about the change? Thinking about all the actors identified above: For the active agents of change, what strategies did they use? (maybe many at one time) For those who facilitated or supported change, did they also use strategies or take part in strategies? For those resisting change, what were their strategies of resistance? Why did they fail? Or did they partially succeed?	Strategies concerning individuals or (non-organised) groups: • Changing individual behaviour (using incentives or threats, making appeals to self-interest, altruism, fear, morality) • Reshaping worldviews/paradigms of understanding (through education, demonstration, dialogue, experience) • Promoting new human relationships through mutual understanding/empathy/reconciliation • Encouraging grassroots participation • Relying on charismatic and visionary leaders, highly networked individuals Strategies concerning institutions and organisations: • Pursuing reform or revolution? • Using coercion or consent? • Working inside or outside of the system? • Taking global/national/local action? • Working for short-term or long-term goals? • Taking legal or illegal action? • Following a top-down or bottom-up strategy? • Creating alliances or encouraging divisions? • Implementing blueprint plans or allowing diversity and experiment? • Forming organisations and movements • Using mass mobilisation/direct action/confronting/challenging • Focusing on organisational learning and flexibility • Empowering people • Providing assistance • Improving communication and information flow • Developing new technologies • Altering the social environment
4. What were the contexts that affected how the change happened? Which contexts *promoted* change?	State context: Regime type, military power, bureaucratic accountability, judicial autonomy, decentralisation, party fragmentation, corruption, history of state formation, political rights, civil war.

ASK YOURSELF…	REMEMBER TO THINK ABOUT…
Which contexts *permitted* change? Which contexts were *barriers* to change? What would a historian say? What would an economist say? A sociologist? Think with a different hat on… Which type of context (state, social, economic, global, environmental, or systemic) do you think was of little relevance to change? Now imagine that it *was* relevant, even important. How could that be so?	Social context: Worldviews and ideologies, nationalism, class structure, gender roles, family structure, religion, urbanisation and housing, cultural autonomy, civil liberties and media freedom, associational life, education/health access and levels, social stability, violence and crime, migration, colonial legacies, trust, social memory, social denial. Economic context: Industrialisation, property distribution, wealth inequality, privatisation, regulation, market access and distortions, corporate power and practice, labour conditions and laws, supply chains, access to technology, infrastructure, inflation, unemployment, macro-economic stability. Global context: Biased international trade rules, commodity price fluctuations, imperialist ambitions, balance of power, interstate conflict, terrorist threats, arms trade, effectiveness of UN institutions, efficacy of international law, Internet access. Environmental context: Geographic differences, resource availability/distribution, climate change, biodiversity, natural disasters, demographics, disease. Systemic context: Power relationships, interdependence, competition, inequality, historical precedents, uncertainty, chance, unknown factors.
5. What was the process or pathway of change? If you could 'draw' the change what would it look like? What kind of pathway did it follow? Change takes place on many levels, so there were probably many simultaneous 'pathways'. How did they interact?	Types of processes: - Cumulative progress/modernisation - Specific sequences, varying pathways, or cycles? - Tipping points - Demonstration effects - Crises or key junctures? - Conflicts or interactions? - Catalysts or cataclysms? - Internal or external pressures? - Systemic self-regulation - Unknown processes
6. Assessing the elements of change Of all the elements you have identified above, which would you pick out as the main ones that led to the change? Were any sufficient alone? Were they all necessary? How did they interact with each other? Which of them do you think is least acknowledged? And for all that has changed, what has not changed?	Some final considerations: - Most processes of change are extremely complex and defy single explanations - You may not have enough information to analyse the change effectively - Beware your personal assumptions and prejudices that affect your analysis - Take into account that your disciplinary speciality or training may still lead you to favour some explanations over others

Note: This is not a model of change; it is a rough guide to thinking through how change has happened in different contexts, from a range of disciplinary perspectives. It is a stimulus to thought rather than a blueprint to follow, a list of possible ingredients rather than a recipe. It makes no attempt to prioritise some aspects of change as being more important than others, nor does it specify how they may interact with each other, or over what time period they operate. The items in parentheses ( ) are examples, not an exhaustive list of the contents of a theme.

Below I provide an example of how the 'rough guide' can help understand and explain a fundamental social change: the abolition of the slave trade and slavery in Britain. It also shows that explanations of social change cannot be easily reduced to a few variables but rather need to draw on a wide range of approaches to change from across different disciplines. This example is not presented as a step-by-step guide to using the 'rough guide'. Rather, it is a narrative produced *after* having used the 'rough guide'.

The abolition of the slave trade and slavery in Britain

According to Alexis de Tocqueville, the abolitionists achieved 'something absolutely without precedent in history…If you pore over the histories of all peoples, I doubt that you will find anything more extraordinary'.

In the 1780s over three-quarters of the world's people were in bondage, across Africa, the Middle East, Asia, Europe, and the Americas. British ships dominated the international slave trade and some half-million African slaves were being worked to death growing sugar cane in British colonies in the West Indies. The idea that slavery was legitimate and 'normal' was deeply entrenched in public consciousness in Britain, and it was generally accepted that the British economy could not survive without slavery and the slave trade. 'If you had proposed, in the London of early 1787, to change all of this,' writes the historian Adam Hochschild, 'nine out of ten people would have laughed you off as a crackpot'.[71] Yet by 1807 the British Parliament had banned the slave trade, and on 1 August 1838, almost 800,000 slaves throughout the British Empire became free, when slavery itself was abolished. How did such a momentous social change take place?

One of the finest recent studies of the reasons for this transformation is Adam Hochschild's *Bury the Chains: The British Struggle to Abolish Slavery* (2006). To what extent does his analysis draw on the themes and categories that appear in 'The rough guide to how change happens'? Hochschild identifies a range of factors, contexts, actors, and strategies which help explain the emergence and success of what he calls the world's 'first great human-rights movement'. Each of them can be traced to one of the elements of the 'rough guide'.

Individual actors

Hochschild's analysis centres on the extraordinary role played by the Anglican deacon Thomas Clarkson, who dedicated his life to the struggle against the slave trade and slavery. Other important actors included a former slave named Olaudah Equiano, whose autobiography became a bestseller, and the parliamentarian William Wilberforce.

Social groups

A variety of social groups were central to the dynamics of change. British plantation owners opposed the abolitionist cause, as did investors in the slave trade, slave-ship captains and workers, and most parliamentarians (especially in the House of Lords). Apart from slaves themselves, the main group in favour of abolition was the Quakers, who had a long history of struggling for their own religious freedom against the state and the established church. Quakers from the business community played a particularly significant role: 'This was the first great social reform movement run mainly by businessmen'.[72]

Human relationships

The abolitionist struggle was conditioned by relationships between these individuals and groups. For instance, Clarkson developed close relations with members of the Quaker community, and had a fifty-year friendship with William Wilberforce, with whom he collaborated to lobby Parliament. The backdrop was the highly unequal and discriminatory feudal relationship that existed between slaves and those who ran the plantations where they laboured.

State, economic, and social context

Obstacles to change were embedded in the institutional context. There were the laws that made slavery and the slave trade legal, and the British Parliament and judiciary which upheld them. There was the international slave trade itself, which was a source of vast profits and employment in the British economy, through its connections to ship-building, insurance, and other industries. All this was situated within the institution of colonialism, which was maintained by the Royal Navy and a culture of racial superiority to the 'primitives' in the British Empire. To challenge the slave trade was to challenge some of the most powerful institutions of the day.

Environmental context

The fact that there was an enormous demand for sugar in Europe, and it could be grown and produced so effectively in the warm climate of the West Indies, was a vital factor in explaining why there was a slave trade at all. The demographic context was also important. High mortality rates among slaves, due to poor conditions on the ships and plantations, lack of medical attention, and inadequate nutrition, meant that more and more slaves were required to replace those who died. It was 'cheaper to buy than to breed', as the saying went.[73]

Forming alliances, mass mobilisation, and media campaigns

'The ultimate success of the movement would be grounded in a series of brilliant alliances', writes Hochschild.[74] The most essential was that between Clarkson and the Quakers. This alliance was the foundation of the mass campaign they mounted from the late 1780s to abolish the slave trade. They used methods that were original in their time but commonplace today. These included: petitions that were presented to Parliament (519 in total), the formation of local committees, and media campaigns (books, pamphlets). Women's organisations, evangelical Christians, and other organisations became involved. People began boycotting Caribbean sugar, one of the first examples of a fair-trade boycott. Plantation owners mounted their own campaign against abolition, and even developed a voluntary code of conduct (common in the corporate world today) in an attempt to convince the public of their concern and compassion for their slaves.

Changing worldviews and tipping points

The abolitionists' strategy of mass mobilisation was part of a concerted effort to shift public thinking so that people in Britain began questioning the legitimacy of the slave trade. By the late 1780s the abolition of the slave trade was the prominent topic in the country's debating societies. Clarkson and his colleagues also distributed 8,700 copies of a diagram of slaves packed on a slave ship, which became a horrific iconic image hung in homes and pubs around Britain. The social action, campaigning, and consciousness-raising by the abolitionists had their effect. The belief among the public that the slave trade should be outlawed spread rapidly throughout the country, with 1788 being a 'tipping point', according to Hochschild.[75] Yet it would still be some years before the political objectives had been achieved.

Reformist change at the national level

It would be wrong to think that the mass mobilisation was part of a radical strategy of achieving change from below. The abolitionists did not encourage rebellion among slaves on ships and plantations, nor did they make much effort to involve the thousands of former slaves in Britain in their campaigns.[76] Mobilisation of public opinion was much more part of a reformist strategy to engage the educated populace, and ultimately to lobby Parliament to achieve change. Clarkson and the Quakers made an early decision not to seek the abolition of slavery outright, but first to aim for the abolition of the slave trade. By some this was seen as an unacceptable compromise, but by others as a realistic and gradualist approach that would be more acceptable to Members of Parliament. Once the slave trade was successfully abolished in 1807, the abolitionists then turned to the issue of slavery. Another reformist strategy was the use of the legal system, for instance to bring cases against slave-ship captains for the murder of slaves.

Empathy

Campaigners against the slave trade and slavery were motivated by many factors, including religious belief, paternalistic pity, and a sense of moral indignation about the violence used against slaves. Yet one of the most original aspects of Hochschild's analysis is the emphasis he places on empathy. 'There is always something mysterious about human empathy, and when we feel it and when we don't', writes Hochschild. The campaign against slavery was 'a sudden upwelling', remarkable for the fact that 'it was the first time a large number of people became outraged, and stayed outraged for many years, over someone else's rights'.[77] The end of slavery in the British Empire cannot be explained without understanding the extraordinary wave of empathy felt among people in Britain for the lives of people of another colour, on another continent.

Crises and junctures

Throughout the 1790s and early 1800s Britain was at war with France. This was accompanied by a wave of repression that effectively stopped all progressive movements in Britain, including abolition. Yet the war ended up providing an opportunity for the abolitionists, through an unlikely association with patriotic sentiments. 'Despite the war', says Hochschild, 'British-owned slave ships, it turned out, were stealthily but profitably supplying slaves to French colonies. Parliament swiftly forbade this, and with the momentum from that move, the abolitionists were able to get both Houses to ban the entire slave trade in 1807'.[78]

Demonstration effects

The abolitionist movement came back to life in the 1820s, partly through the work of Clarkson and the establishment of over 70 'ladies'' anti-slavery societies. The news of the revived movement spread across the Atlantic and contributed to sparking an uprising of over 20,000 Jamaican slaves in 1831. The rebellion helped convince the British establishment that the cost of continued slavery was too high. In 1838, after another mass wave of petitions and demonstrations, slavery in the British Empire was finally abolished.

This example of the British struggle against slavery demonstrates how the 'rough guide' can be a tool to help comprehend and explain social change. First, the various elements of Hochschild's study can all be situated and organised within the categories and themes of the guide, providing an analytical overview of a dense historical narrative. Second, it is clear that explaining abolition requires drawing on approaches to change from many disciplines, including sociological theories of worldviews, psychologists' insights into human motivation, political science concepts such as demonstration effects, and historical ideas such as key junctures. Third, it facilitates identifying those areas that do not play a major role in his analysis, for instance the use of revolutionary and illegal strategies (which were, in contrast, central to the successful slave revolt in the French colony of San Domingo in the 1790s).

More generally, this analytical summary brings out two important lessons for human development. First, the success of the abolitionists in the face of extreme obstacles to change (such as the power of plantation owners, the intransigence of Parliament, and the overwhelming public support for slavery) provides hope for those attempting to reduce poverty and inequality in regions such as sub-Saharan Africa, who are confronted by similarly daunting obstacles. Second, it might appear almost impossible to convince wealthy consumers in the North to care about poverty in the South, yet the struggle against slavery highlights the conditions and strategies that may indeed make it possible to mobilise people in favour of somebody else's rights in a distant country.[79]

Part 3: Approaches to change in contemporary development thinking

Development organisations such as Oxfam see change as their core activity, but to what extent does contemporary development thinking about how to tackle poverty and inequality draw upon the full range of approaches to change discussed in this paper? Do development theorists and analysts think about change like, for instance, economists, political scientists, or behavioural psychologists? Or do they have their own distinctive perspectives on how change happens, which defy the approaches of other disciplines? This section attempts to answer these questions through reviewing a sample of prevalent development strategies adopted by a disparate range of development actors, including international financial organisations such as the World Bank, bilateral aid donors, and NGOs. The strategies discussed are not comprehensive, and vary widely between different kinds of development players, but offer a representative selection of the approaches currently found in these organisations. They also reflect approaches to change that appear in the interdisciplinary subject of development studies.

The analysis begins by examining the neo-liberal approach of *market liberalisation*. This is contrasted with the *managed markets* strategy which has become popular among development organisations who advocate fair trade rather than embracing neo-liberal free trade. *Corporate social responsibility* is analysed as a third approach to development that focuses primarily on the economic sphere. Following is a discussion of *international aid* as a response to poverty and inequality. I then turn to the idea of *empowerment*, which takes four main forms: satisfying fundamental needs, rights-based approaches, capabilities, and empowering women. Closely related are the bottom-up strategies of *grassroots participation and social organisation*. After examining development through *reforming the state* I shift to *land reform and securing private property*. The final strategy subject to analysis is that of *changing attitudes and beliefs*.

Needless to say there are major debates within the development community as to which strategy or combination of strategies deserves priority, with scholars, government agencies, development NGOs, and other civil-society organisations in both the North and South favouring different approaches and combinations. The purpose of this section is not to adjudicate between them but to place them in intellectual context with respect to their assumptions about how change happens.

Market liberalisation

There are two major market-oriented development strategies. First is the free-market neo-liberal approach favoured by economists such as Jagdish Bhagwati, and put into practice through the IMF, the World Bank, and the WTO. Among the main elements are privatisation of state utilities, the removal of import tariffs and barriers to foreign direct investment, the promotion of export-led growth, and liberalisation in the service sector.[80] Economic growth is seen as the engine of development, and the private sector and international trade the most effective vehicles for achieving it. A business-friendly environment with free markets will hence promote pro-poor growth. Bhagwati is fond of ridiculing ideas such as 'fair trade' in favour of market liberalisation.[81] While his neo-liberal arguments frequently appear in the press, they have minimal support among those working in the majority of development agencies and organisations.

This development strategy derives primarily from within the confines of classical liberal economics, which is rooted in the writings of thinkers such as Adam Smith, Friedrich Hayek, and Joseph Schumpeter. Ideas including the invisible hand, comparative advantage, and rational self-interested actors are taken as fundamental axioms. The approach incorporates elements of behavioural psychology, particularly the notion that behaviour can be changed by altering incentive structures and appealing to self-interest. The stress on self-interest and competition has parallels with approaches to change in Darwinist evolutionary biology. There is also a close link with modernisation theory, since many neo-liberals argue that the spread of wealth through the operation of the free market will gradually help political power spread among citizens and contribute to the development of liberal democracy. The assumption that wealth created by firms can 'trickle down' to poor people accords with top-down approaches to change. As discussed above, free-market economics has become effectively ahistorical through its retreat into theoretical and mathematical modelling. Most neo-liberal theories ignore issues that are fundamental in many disciplines such as: the role of power in society; the effect of economic and social inequality on the operation of markets and access to markets; that individuals are motivated by many things apart from rational self-interest; and that behaviour is shaped by worldviews. This confirms the intellectual and empirical isolation of free-market development strategies.

Managed markets

An alternative market-focused strategy agrees that international trade can help bring people out of poverty, but argues that the existing rules and practices of the global trade system, in addition to market distortions, limit the benefits that poor countries and people can gain from trade. Changes required include: improving developing-country access to developed-country markets through reducing or eradicating rich-country import barriers and subsidies, particularly for agriculture; increasing developing-country voice in the decision-making processes of the WTO, and making the WTO more transparent and accountable; and allowing developing countries to protect key industries from foreign competition in order to consolidate their development, just as European countries did from the 1880s. These are the kinds of changes advocated by development thinkers such as Martin Khor and organisations including Oxfam and ActionAid in their efforts to 'make trade fair'.[82] Such policies have been analysed from a historical perspective in Ha-Joon Chang's *Kicking Away the Ladder* (2002) and in his more recent paper 'Why Developing Countries Need Tariffs' (2005).

The managed-markets strategy is an exemplary reformist approach to social change. It accepts the neo-liberal faith in markets and that change must take place within the general framework of a capitalist global economy. But it challenges the idea that market liberalisation benefits the poor. It draws on some of the heterodox economic policies advocated by economists such as Dani Rodrik. It is sensitive to problems of power, such as how the power of corporations or rich countries can distort markets. The solutions of new rules and systems, and increased participation and accountability, are familiar to political scientists who stress the importance of institutional change. The belief that such institutional reforms at the global level could successfully make trade fair reflects an optimism that appears in idealist theories of international relations. The argument that poor countries should be permitted to protect themselves or enjoy 'special measures' under the WTO echoes the Marxist-inspired dependency theories of the 1970s (such as Immanuel Wallerstein's 'world systems theory'), which highlighted the unequal relationship between the wealthy 'centre' and the poorer 'periphery' of the global capitalist system.

Corporate social responsibility

Corporate social responsibility (CSR) has become one of the watchwords of contemporary development strategy. Organisations such as AccountAbility publish regular reports on how CSR and 'responsible business practice' are transforming global markets and contributing to economic and social development.[83] Part of the CSR argument is that it is possible to shift the behaviour of corporations through appealing to their self-interest, for instance by convincing major supermarket chains of the benefits of widening their appeal to 'ethical consumers', or by threatening their reputation with name and shame campaigns so that they undertake practices that promote development. Oxfam's report, 'Trading Away Our Rights: Women Working in Global Supply Chains', highlights the benefits and challenges of promoting ethical purchasing practices in fresh produce and clothing supply chains to help make trade work for women workers, their families, and communities.[84] A recent ActionAid paper, 'Power Hungry: Six Reasons to Regulate Global Food Corporations', emphasises the limited scope and effectiveness of voluntary CSR codes.[85]

Working with selected powerful companies is an example of making alliances with progressive élites, which appears in the social-movement and civil-society literature as a strategy of change. It reflects a reformist approach to development based on operating within the existing capitalist economic system. It also exhibits a strategy of change coming 'from above', although there is a 'from below' element in the sense that firms may be responsive to consumer pressure to act more ethically, and because most NGOs combine their CSR work with promoting worker organisations and public-awareness campaigns. Finding companies that have been both economically successful and socially responsible, and using them as exemplars to encourage the spread of CSR, is an instance of relying on demonstration effects as an approach to change. Historians of corporations could point out that there is little precedent for companies taking moral stances except insofar as it contributes to profits or shareholder value. They might also note that ethical initiatives from the private sector have more often come from individual philanthropists (such as Rockefeller, Gates) than from corporate entities themselves.[86]

International aid

Aid is a key tool in the strategies of governments and development organisations. International aid gives developing countries opportunities to provide basic education and health care, strengthen institutions, increase aggregate savings, investment and growth, stabilise countries after shocks (such as conflict, famine, earthquakes) and contribute to long-term poverty reduction more generally.[87] Books such as William Easterly's *The White Man's Burden: Why the West's Efforts to Aid the Rest Have Done so Much Ill and So Little Good* (2006) have stirred controversy about the efficacy of international aid but have been met with harsh rebuttals by development thinkers including Amartya Sen.[88] Two major debates are whether to increase absolute levels of aid, and how to make aid more effective. Other areas of debate include whether government aid should be tied or untied, and multilateral or bilateral.

International aid is an acknowledgement that certain institutional and environmental contexts and problems are fundamental obstacles to pursuing development strategies (of whatever form). These contexts might be drought induced by climate change, enormous debt burdens, an HIV and AIDS crisis, an absence of resources such as coal or oil, or a lack of infrastructure following its destruction in civil war. This focus on contexts of change is familiar to sociologists and anthropologists, rather than neo-liberal economists who are eager to impose their models for change without a full appreciation of the contextual limitations and social realities. A strategy of providing international aid embraces the ideas of modernisation theory and the Enlightenment, in that aid helps countries put their first foot on the ladder of development, which they will then be able to climb. Raising aid from citizens in wealthy countries is often based on appeal to psychological traits such as shame, empathy, or a sense of justice.

Empowerment

The idea of empowerment is central to four main strands of development thinking: satisfying fundamental needs, rights-based approaches, capabilities, and empowering women.

First, the bedrock of most contemporary development policy is that satisfying people's needs in areas such as health and education helps to empower individuals, with broad-reaching consequences for development. For example, providing education for girls has been shown to have a profound impact on their political freedom, gender equality, income poverty reduction, effective population policies, and family health.[89] This development strategy features prominently, for instance, in Jeffrey Sachs's *The End of Poverty* and is implicit in the Millennium Development Goals.[90] The idea of development through meeting fundamental needs reflects the assumption in modernisation theory that change is cumulative, with each stage in development contributing to future stages. It also echoes the Enlightenment's faith in the possibility of progress and human advancement, the idea of evolutionary change found in the natural sciences, and represents a bottom-up approach to change. The focus is very much on linear processes of change, with insufficient appreciation of varying pathways or sequences of development, or that existing power structures can provide significant obstacles to change.

Rights-based approaches to development usually contain two elements. First, that international human-rights conventions (for example ILO Convention 169 on indigenous rights) should be incorporated into national law. This is effectively a top-down and legalistic strategy that accords with the focus on rights (individual, group, human) that appears in legal studies and moral philosophy. A second element is that, at the local level, people should be informed of their rights and empowered to exercise them. What they may have previously considered 'needs' can be understood as 'rights' (such as the right to health care) that can be claimed from the state.[91] This approach implies a degree of social mobilisation from below and the idea of government accountability to citizens, prominent in the political science literature. It also concerns changing people's worldviews about their legitimate claims on the state.

Amartya Sen's 'capabilities' approach to development also concerns empowerment, in that it advocates that individuals should be given the opportunity to strengthen and expand their capabilities to lead the kind of life that they value (for example to be free from disease, take part in community life, or have self-respect).[92] The capabilities approach moves beyond traditional economist assumptions that individuals are rational actors pursuing their self-interest, or they all want to have the same basic needs fulfilled, to a more sociological acknowledgement that individuals may value different things and wish to pursue a variety of goals. That is, people want to be empowered to enjoy a range of freedoms.

Finally, the empowerment of women has become one of the key goals of development interventions, and involves ensuring that women have the ability to make strategic life choices where this ability was previously denied (for example through access to resources and involvement in decision-making).[93] Such thinking can be traced back to the increasing focus since the 1960s on women's rights, experiences, and histories across a range of academic disciplines such as sociology, political science, and history, and to the rise of feminist economics.

Grassroots participation and social organisation

Grassroots participation and social organisation comprise distinct yet related approaches to development. With respect to the former, in the past 20 years there has been an increasing emphasis on development policies that embrace and promote participation from people in poor communities. Closely linked to the idea of empowering individuals, it has taken many forms, such as participatory poverty assessments, participatory learning and action (PLA), and action research, and has been adopted as standard practice by lenders, donors, international NGOs, and governments, as discussed in the writings of Robert Chambers.[94] Successful examples of participatory local development, such as the Panchayati Raj system in India (which has a strong element of decentralisation), have become models for this development strategy.[95] While grassroots participation can focus on the local level, it can also be directed towards changes at the national and global level. An underlying assumption of many participatory approaches is not only that participation is an ethical imperative and right, but that poor people are best placed to come up with solutions to their own development problems.

In what ways does grassroots participation draw on approaches to change discussed in Part 1 of this paper? Involving members of poor communities in decisions that affect their lives has parallels with twentieth-century theories of direct democracy, which stress the importance of direct participation by citizens in political life, and strategies of change from below.[96] Participatory development strategies can also be traced back to the participatory emphasis in community-development studies and popular education movements of the 1960s and 1970s, which themselves were often rooted in Marxism (such as the writings of Paulo Friere).[97] The publication of studies such as *Voices of the Poor: Can Anyone Hear Us?* (2000), by Deepa Narayan *et al.* for the World Bank, which uses individual testimony extensively, demonstrates that the anthropological and sociological approach of prioritising the experiences and ideas of ordinary people has become mainstream.

Related to the strategy of grassroots participation is that change is achieved through social organisation and mass mobilisation from below. This could take the form of social movements, mass demonstrations, or other forms of collective action. The aim is usually to generate the political pressure required to change government policy or laws, to implement promises or obligations, and to redistribute political, economic, and social power to those in need. It is reflected in the idea that one of the major roles of civil society is to hold governments to account for their actions. An example of such social mobilisation is the mass demonstrations at the G8 summit in Edinburgh in 2005 as part of the UK Make Poverty History campaign, comprising a coalition of over 500 organisations.

The strategy of building coalitions between organisations relates to social-movement theory and civil-society analyses that stress the importance of making alliances between different social sectors. Much social-movement activity effectively incorporates the idea of 'tipping points' through the belief that if you get a critical mass of people onto the streets it can 'tip' governments to make major policy shifts. A further element of collective protest strategies is that mass action at one point in time can trigger more action in the future or in other locations, which is the essence of the 'demonstration effect' phenomenon familiar to political scientists. To the extent that mass mobilisation is aimed at changing or implementing laws or government policies, it embodies the idea of reformist change from below rather than revolutionary change.

Reforming the state

There are two major schools of thought concerning the role of the state in development. One is the 'good governance' approach, which assumes that states can become neutral entities with the potential to make a major contribution to development. Changes required include: governments taking more responsibility for development policy rather than having it dictated by the international community; solving endemic problems such as corruption, which hamper the development process; providing effective leadership; improving administrative efficiency and capacity to ensure effective policy implementation and monitoring; and decentralisation. A focus on good governance as the key to development is central to the UK Department for International Development's recent White Paper, 'Eliminating World Poverty: Making Governance Work for the Poor' (July 2006). A second approach might be called the 'malign power' school of thought. Here the assumption is that states reflect the power inequalities in society and are a haven for élites and deeply entrenched clientelistic practices. Administrative reforms of the 'good governance' style must be complemented with challenging the power of state élites and enhancing government accountability to poor citizens. Many of these issues are put into context in Matthew Lockwood's *The State They're In: An Agenda for International Action on Poverty in Africa* (2005).[98]

The resurgence of thinking about the state's role in development in the past decade comes as a surprise to many political scientists and political sociologists (especially those on the left), who wonder why the focus of attention in development thinking ever shifted from the nation-state in the first place. The revival of state-centred development approaches is partly an acknowledgement that the world may indeed have become global, but that governments still play a major role in the lives of their citizens, particularly through policy implementation. (The revival is also a response to international financial institution policy failures in the 1980s.) The growing concern with corruption in development circles since the 1990s resembles political sociologists' interest in corruption, clientelism, and patronage in developing and developed countries since the 1960s. The emphasis on 'good governance' for development parallels the rise of the 'new institutionalism' in political science, with its stress on the importance of designing effective and transparent political institutions, and shares with it a reformist approach to change.

Land reform and securing private property

Land-related development strategies currently focus on two areas: redistributive land reform; and ensuring security of land tenure.

Redistribution of land through agrarian reform has a long history as a development strategy. Land reform can help give landless populations the opportunity to ensure food security through growing their own crops, provide them somewhere to build a home, allow indigenous people to reclaim lands that they have historically occupied, and reduce the economic and political power of landed élites. While acknowledging that agrarian reforms are not always successful, some development organisations continue to highlight 'success stories' such as Taiwan and South Korea, which demonstrate how land reform was an essential basis for their development.[99] The mass protests and occupations by Brazil's Landless Rural Workers Movement (Movimento dos Trabalhadores Rurais Sem Terra, MST) demonstrate the contemporary relevance of land reform as a development strategy. However, the rise of urbanisation and the growth of service economies in many poor countries have made agrarian reform a less pressing issue for some development analysts, especially given the fact that significant land reforms have usually only taken place during periods of major political upheaval.

The fact that land reform remains on some development agendas as a means of tackling rural poverty and challenging the power of large landowners is a recognition that the analysis of inequality and class – which was at its height among historians and social scientists in the 1970s – still has a place in development studies. It also demonstrates a respect for the conclusions of those historical sociologists who argue that representative democracy, and economic and social development, have rarely emerged in contexts of highly unequal land ownership and labour-repressive agricultural systems controlled by a rural oligarchy.

A variation on the land-reform strategy appears in Hernando De Soto's *The Mystery of Capital: Why Capitalism Triumphs in the West and Fails Everywhere Else* (2000). He argues that poor people often have assets – land which they occupy illegally and the house they built on it (for instance in a shanty town) – but that such assets are 'dead' because, being outside the formal property system, they cannot be used as collateral to help get bank loans and mortgages. This means they are unable to obtain the capital that allows entrepreneurs to set up new businesses and which gives capitalist development its driving force. His solution is to encourage governments to formalise the property holdings of poor people by granting them legal title to their occupied property. That is, the key to development lies in empowering people through security of private property.[100]

De Soto's approach to development exists within a neo-liberal economic context that reinforces the institution of individual private property. This is also reflected in his explicit statements that the private property of the wealthy must be left intact in any property-reform process, which is similar to the political science 'transitology' approach to change. His stress on improving the administrative efficiency and effectiveness of the property titling system displays a concern with bureaucratic processes and responsiveness evident in the political science literature on institutional reform. A major criticism is that he fails to address issues of power. For instance, much illegal property occupation in developing countries is of privately-held land, yet it is not clear how legal titles to such land could be granted by the state without challenging the power of entrenched élites who may own such property and frequently use private and state force to protect it. In general, De Soto's argument is a classic single-solution or 'magic bullet' development formula that takes insufficient account of social, economic, and political contexts.

Approaches to securing property rights have not been monopolised by De Soto. A recent study by the International Institute for Environment and Development provides examples of innovative and effective policies (such as land-titling programmes) in countries such as Ethiopia, Mozambique, and Niger, which have ensured land-tenure security in poor communities.[101] This and other analyses highlight land-tenure and ownership problems faced by women, who often do not enjoy the same property rights as men, for example in Kenya.[102] Unlike De Soto's arguments, these analyses recognise issues of power inequalities and that communal land holdings may be just as important as individual private property.

Changing attitudes and beliefs

Altering people's behaviour through shifting their attitudes and beliefs is a significant contemporary development strategy, especially for campaigning organisations. One strategy is to focus on changing the attitudes and beliefs of people in their capacity as consumers or citizens. This can take the form, for instance, of public campaigns to promote buying fair-trade products or taking educational materials to schools. A second strategy is to concentrate on changing the beliefs of élites and policy makers. Immersion programmes run by the World Bank and other development agencies provide an example. In the World Bank's 'Grass Roots Immersion Program' (GRIP) and 'Village Immersion Program' (VIP), international staff spend up to a week living with a poor family in a rural or urban area in a developing country. The participants often help with tasks such as cooking or crop harvesting, and have opportunities to discuss daily life with their host families. According to one participant in the UK Department for International Development (DFID) immersion programme, the immersion helped create the 'ability to put into words the perceptions of poorer people and more ability to empathise with their perspective'.[103]

Changing attitudes and beliefs moves beyond the approaches in economics and psychology that focus on altering people's behaviour through providing incentives that appeal to their existing self-interest. It is a deeply sociological strategy that draws on ideas such as worldviews, consent, and ideology: changing the way people think is an effective way of changing what they do. Immersion programmes resemble approaches to change that emphasise the importance of building personal relationships and having new experiences as a means of developing mutual understanding and empathy. Changing people's attitudes and beliefs is a long-term approach to development which contrasts with or can be an important complement to less profound yet more immediately visible short-term strategies such as passing new laws, changing government practices, or redesigning state institutions.

These various development strategies, and their relationship to the factors and processes in the 'rough guide', are summarised in the table below.

DEVELOPMENT STRATEGY	UNDERLYING APPROACH TO HOW CHANGE HAPPENS
Market liberalisation	This corresponds with ideas of rational self-interest, the invisible hand, and the free self-regulating market in classical economics, and reflects theories of human motivation and competition from behavioural psychology and Darwinian evolutionary biology. 'Trickle-down' development is a top-down approach to social change. Market-liberalisation theories are insensitive to problems of unequal power and inequality in society.
Managed markets	This is a reformist strategy deriving from heterodox economic thinking and dependency theory. It contains an awareness of how powerful actors (such as corporations) can distort markets. Advocating improved accountability and participation in global institutions echoes liberal democratic theories in political science and reflects an optimism about institutional change that appears in idealist international-relations thinking.
Corporate social responsibility	This is another reformist approach to change based on operating within the existing capitalist economic system. It may require working with progressive élites, a strategy appearing in social-movement and civil-society theory. It contains ideas of demonstration effects common in studies of social-movement cycles, and political science analyses of 'waves' of regime change and 'domino effects'.
International aid	This strategy is sensitive to institutional and environmental contexts that can hamper change. The idea that aid can help countries put their first foot on the ladder of development is a linear approach to change corresponding to modernisation theory and Enlightenment ideas. It shows a faith in the possibilities of global co-operation evident in idealist thinking in international relations, and the psychological assumption that wealthy citizens in the North can empathise with poorer citizens in the South.
Empowerment	*Satisfying needs*: This reflects modernisation theory, ideas of change through cumulative progress, evolutionary theories in the natural sciences, and bottom-up strategies of change. It is a linear approach insensitive to varying sequences and pathways of change, or to obstacles such as the power of entrenched élites. *Rights-based approaches*: This is a legalistic approach with both top-down and bottom-up elements. It implies a degree of change through social mobilisation and education. It is based on ideas of accountability appearing in political science. *Capabilities*: This strategy moves beyond the rational choice and self-interest assumptions of classical economics and embraces sociological ideas such as that people value different things and wish to pursue a variety of goals. *Empowering women*: This reflects the rise of gendered approaches in history, economics, sociology, and other disciplines since the 1960s, which themselves draw on a recognition of women's political and social struggles since the nineteenth century.
Grassroots participation and social organisation	*Grassroots participation*: This contains ideas of participatory democracy, direct democracy, and decentralisation from political science, and change from below evident in Marxist history. Listening to people's voices draws on thinking from social anthropology, sociology, and oral history. *Social organisation*: This strategy appears in social-movement theory and is generally a form of reformist change from below, sensitive to problems of political power. It recognises the role of tipping points and demonstration effects, and the importance of making coalitions across social divides.

Reforming the state	This is a reformist approach to change familiar to political scientists from the 'new institutionalism' school who advocate 'good governance' and focusing policy change on state institutions. The importance of tackling corruption is a theme recognised by political sociologists as a major factor in achieving social change.
Land reform and securing private property	*Land reform*: This strategy is often advocated by leftist thinkers concerned with class and inequality who argue that positive change requires redistributing economic resources. It also reflects thinking amongst historical sociologists who show that development and democracy have rarely emerged in conditions of extreme land inequality. *Securing private property*: This is a more legalistic approach to change emphasising the liberal democratic idea of property rights, and the importance of bureaucratic efficiency that appears in political-science writing on institutional state reform.
Changing attitudes and beliefs	This is a long-term strategy which moves beyond the assumptions of rational self-interested actors in economics and behavioural psychology to a more sociological emphasis on the importance of worldviews, ideology, and consent as determinants of human motivation and action. It focuses on building personal relationships, mutual understanding, and empathy as an approach to change, as well as reframing dominant paradigms.

Conclusions

How do the development strategies in the above section relate to the range of disciplinary approaches summarised in the 'rough guide'? My main observation is that, for all their richness, these development strategies closely resemble or are derived from within the realm of approaches to change that have emerged in history, politics, sociology, and other areas of academic inquiry. The strategies of change prevalent among development organisations or within the field of development studies more generally are far from unique.

But is development thinking drawing on the full range of approaches to change summarised in the 'rough guide'? Clearly not. Despite their diversity and creativity, the development strategies I have discussed share five main limitations.

Excessive reformism without politics or history: Mainstream development thinking is essentially reformist, attempting to work within existing institutions and systems. There is little of the radical thought that could be found among development theorists and organisations in the 1970s, when dependency theory reigned. Issues of power and inequality – that remain central in disciplines such as sociology – are often downplayed. Many contemporary development strategies are composed primarily of politically neutral and historical ideas such as 'good governance', 'institutional reform', and 'regulating markets'. Yet disregarding the underlying distribution of power and structure of inequality not only means that important obstacles to change are not addressed; it also reveals a bias towards maintaining the status quo. Development organisations limited to a reformist agenda would have found it difficult to support the African National Congress during Apartheid because of their policy of armed struggle, or to support over two decades of illegal land occupations by Brazil's Landless Rural Workers Movement, one of the world's most successful social movements.

Possible questions to ask to overcome this limitation:

Are there ways of working outside the system? For example, how could policies of institutional reform in Brazil be combined with a more radical approach to tackling inequality?

Disregarding the environment: Most development strategies fail to situate their approach in an environmental framework. By ignoring the environment, the strategies are insensitive to the environmental impact of the changes they seek, and hence the consequent repercussions on development. It is becoming increasingly clear that all strategies must take into account factors such as climate change, the loss of biodiversity, and the interdependence of ecological systems. Development studies and environmental science must merge into an ecological humanism in order to ensure the change they seek.

Possible questions to ask to overcome this limitation:

What are the environmental impacts and repercussions of our strategy? For example, what could an environmental scientist contribute to our discussions about new housing projects in India?

Overlooking personal relationships and mutual understanding: Development strategies display an overwhelming focus on individual actors, organised social groups, and institutions, with little acknowledgement that societies and institutions are composed of human relationships that are a potential locus of change. Immersion programmes that involve shared experience and conversation between people who know little about each other's lives are a rare exception. There is much greater scope for development organisations to pursue strategies that encourage mutual understanding, empathy, and trust by creating personal relationships between those who have and those who have not, and which contribute to changing the attitudes and beliefs of those in power.

Possible questions to ask to overcome this limitation:

What kinds of conversation and dialogue are needed, and between whom? For example, how can we build in a process of *personal* dialogue for greater empathy between donors, government representatives, and the local community as part of an education workshop in Nairobi?

Underestimating contextual limitations: The 'rough guide' highlights an enormous number of contextual factors that affect change or are an obstacle to it. These include institutional contexts such as party fragmentation, levels of migration, and religion. The development strategies discussed in this paper tend to underestimate the importance of such contexts, and hence overestimate the possibilities for successful change. Development in the West has taken place in very specific historical contexts and sequences, as well as over a long period, and it may be almost impossible to replicate such development except in exceptional circumstances.

Possible questions to ask to overcome this limitation:

How will state, social, economic, global, and systemic contexts affect our development strategy? For example, which worldviews are the greatest obstacle to its success and how could we change them?

Lack of multidisciplinary agility: Most development strategies rally around a single change factor or a limited range of factors (such as De Soto's idea that development problems can be largely solved through property-titling programmes), and fail to respond to the lessons of change learned in domains outside development studies. As the example of the abolition of the slave trade and slavery in Britain illustrates, fundamental social change is usually a product of a range of strategic approaches associated with many different disciplines. There is an acute need for greater multidisciplinary agility when thinking about development and designing new strategies and programmes. One of the main reasons why economists such as Jeffrey Sachs are enthusiastic about Jared Diamond is because Diamond is not an economist: he provides original insights into development issues through approaching them from the perspective of geography, behavioural ecology, and other disciplines.

Possible questions to ask to overcome this limitation:

How could our disciplinary approach be broadened? For example, are there people in our organisation from different disciplinary backgrounds whose talents and insights could be drawn upon?

Overall, the message of this paper is simple. There are many ways in which social change has happened and could happen. We should not allow ourselves to become trapped by our disciplinary assumptions, specialist knowledge, or habitual approaches. We should have the courage to be creative in the way we think about explaining and promoting change.

This paper is an invitation to consider how the change you are interested in could be approached and understood from the perspective of different disciplines or thinkers. How would a political scientist or an anthropologist or a social psychologist explain the success of a health project you worked on in Viet Nam? How important were government decisions compared to the emotional landscape of individuals? Should you search for the explanations of success over the past two years or be a historian and examine the past two hundred years? What would Jared Diamond or Malcolm Gladwell or Vandana Shiva or Theodore Zeldin say about the issue? What would a shanty-town dweller you once met in Rio say about it? How does this compare with your own views?

When Mahatma Gandhi was asked if he was a Hindu he replied, 'Yes I am, I am also a Muslim, a Christian, a Buddhist, and a Jew.' When you are asked, for instance, if you are a development analyst, you could answer, 'Yes I am, but I also strive to be a historian, an anthropologist, a sociologist, a political scientist…'

A final thought. This analysis has focused on how change happens. Yet the history of human societies has been as much about continuity as about change. Commenting on the apparent transformation of French society brought about by events in 1848, Marx wrote that the old governmental and military system 'continued to exist inviolate' and that where the constitution changed, 'the change concerned the table of contents, not the contents; the name, not the subject matter'.[104] Wherever we look for what has changed, we should also look for what has stayed the same.

Endnotes

1 E. H. Carr (1987) *What is History?*, Harmondsworth, UK: Penguin: 87.

2 Quoted in E. H. Carr (1987: 49).

3 E. Hobsbawm (1998) *The Age of Empire 1975–1914*, London: Weidenfeld and Nicolson: 188.

4 K. Marx and F. Engels (1974) *The German Ideology*, London: Lawrence and Wishart: 64.

5 E. Hobsbawm (1997: 188).

6 K. Marx (1954) *The Eighteenth Brumaire of Louis Bonaparte*, Moscow: Progress Publishers and London: Lawrence and Wishart: 19.

7 D. Reuschmeyer, E. H. Stephens, and J. D. Stephens (1992) *Capitalist Development and Democracy*, Cambridge: Polity Press: 72.

8 E. H. Carr (1987: 37–40).

9 N. Elias and E. Dunning (1986) *Quest for Excitement: Sport and Leisure in the Civilizing Process*, Oxford: Blackwell: 34–5.

10 E. P. Thompson (1968) *The Making of the English Working Class*, Harmondsworth, UK: Pelican: 13.

11 Colley quoted in K. Faulks (1998) *Citizenship in Modern Britain*, Edinburgh: Edinburgh University Press: 105.

12 A. Gramsci (1971) *Selections from the Prison Notebooks*, London: Lawrence and Wishart: 210.

13 Quoted in E. H. Carr (1987: 98).

14 E. H. Carr (1987: 102).

15 F. Fanon (1963) *The Wretched of the Earth*, New York: Grove Press: 35.

16 M. Smith (1995) 'Pluralism', in D. Marsh and G. Stoker (eds.) *Theory and Method in Political Science*, Basingstoke and London: Macmillan: 210.

17 M. Mann (1993) *The Sources of Social Power, Volume 2: The rise of classes and nation-states, 1760–1914*, Cambridge: Cambridge University Press: 45, 47, 48, 55, 65.

18 M. De Landa (1997) *A Thousand Years of Nonlinear History*, New York: Zone Books.

19 J. J. Linz and A. Stepan (1996) *Problems of Democratic Transition and Consolidation: Southern Europe, South America, and Post-Communist Europe*, Baltimore and London: Johns Hopkins University Press: 56–60.

20 B. Moore (1973) *Social Origins of Dictatorship and Democracy: Lord and Peasant in the Making of the Modern World*, Harmondsworth, UK: Penguin University Books: 418, 413–14.

21 W. L. Miller (1995) 'Quantitative Methods', in D. Marsh and G. Stoker (eds.) *Theory and Method in Political Science*, Basingstoke and London: Macmillan: 160–1.

22 On ideas, signs, and symbols of freedom in the USA, see M. Foley (1991) *American Political Ideas: Traditions and Usages*, Manchester: Manchester University Press: Chapter 1.

23 E. Hobsbawm (1987: 102).

24 B. Anderson (1991) *Imagined Communities: Reflections on the Origin and Spread of Nationalism*, London: Verso.

[25] C. W. Mills (1970 [1956]) *The Power Elite*, New York: Oxford University Press: 45.

[26] M. Weber (1968: 1006) *Economy and Society: An Outline of Interpretive Sociology*, G. Roth and C. Wittich (eds.) New York: Bedminster Press.

[27] See also J. Foweraker and R. Krznaric (2002) 'The Uneven Performance of Third Wave Democracies: Electoral Politics and the Imperfect Rule of Law in Latin America', Latin American Politics and Society 44(3): 44–6.

[28] R. A. Dahl (1989) *Democracy and its Critics*, New Haven and London: Yale University Press: 130–31; D. Held (1996) *Models of Democracy*, Cambridge: Polity Press: 245–47; S. Bowles and H. Gintis (1986) *Democracy and Capitalism: Property, Community and the Contradictions of Modern Social Thought*, London: Routledge & Kegan Paul: 3.

[29] For a more detailed analysis and theoretical conceptualisation of this latter issue, see J. Gaventa (October 2006) 'Finding the Space for Change: A Power Analysis', IDS Bulletin: Exploring Power for Change 37(6). See also the discussion in Just Associates et al. (2006) 'Making Change Happen: Citizen Engagement and Global Economic Power', http://www.justassociates.org/publications_files/MCH2.pdf.

[30] See also P. Kropotkin (1998 [1902]) *Mutual Aid: A Factor of Evolution*, London: Freedom Press and M. Buber (1949) *Paths in Utopia*, London: Routledge & Kegan Paul.

[31] Mannheim (1997 [1952]) refers to the idea of Weltanschaung, whereas Bourdieu (1990) discusses worldviews through the concept of the 'habitus'.

[32] R. Krznaric (2003) 'The Worldview of the Oligarchy in Guatemalan Politics', Ph.D thesis, University of Essex (UK); R. Krznaric (2007, forthcoming) 'What the Rich Don't Tell the Poor: Conversations in Guatemala', Guatemala City: Inforpress Centroamericana.

[33] D. Goleman (1996) *Emotional Intelligence: Why It Can Matter More Than IQ*, London: Bloomsbury: 106–10.

[34] S. R. Clegg (1989) *Frameworks of Power*, London: Sage: 153.

[35] For a discussion of dimensions of power, see Clegg (1989: Chapter 5).

[36] A. Krog (1998) *Country of My Skull*, London: Jonathan Cape.

[37] M. Casaus Arzú (1992) *Guatemala: Linaje y Racismo*, San José, Costa Rica: FLASCO; R. Krznaric (2006) 'The Limits of Pro-poor Agricultural Trade in Guatemala: Land, Labour and Political Power', Journal of Human Development 7(1): 120–23.

[38] A. Kohn (1990) *The Brighter Side of Human Nature: Altruism and Empathy in Everyday Life*, New York: Basic Books: 49–50.

[39] S. Freud (1996 [1900]) *The Interpretation of Dreams*, New York: Gramercy Books: vii; C. Jung (1964) *Man and His Symbols*, London: Picador.

[40] T. N. Hanh (1987) *Being Peace*, London: Rider: 61–80.

[41] The culture of fear generated around the war on terror is discussed by sociologist Barry Glassner at http://www.buzzflash.com/interviews/03/04/10_glassner.html. See also B. Glassner (2000) *The Culture of Fear: Why Americans are Afraid of the Wrong Things*, New York: Basic Books.

[42] S. Cohen (2001) *States of Denial: Knowing about Atrocities and Suffering*, Cambridge: Polity Press: 266–77.

[43] A. Sen (1977) 'Rational Fools: A critique of the behavioural foundations of economic thought', Philosophy and Public Affairs 6(4): 317–44.

[44] D. Rodrik (2004) 'Rethinking Growth Policies in the Developing World', Cambridge MA: Harvard University: 2.

[45] D. Rodrik (2004: 3–10).

[46] D. Elson (ed.) (1991) *Male Bias in the Development Process*, Manchester: Manchester University Press.; D. Budlender and G. Hewitt (eds.) (2002) *Gender Budgets Make More Cents: Country Studies and Good Practice*, London: Commonwealth Secretariat. Special thanks to Thalia Kidder from Oxfam GB for assistance with this section.

[47] C. W. Mills (1956); C. E. Lindblom (1983) 'The Privileged Position of Business', in M. Green (ed.), *The Big Business Reader on Corporate America*, New York: Pilgrim Press: 193–203; N. Chomsky (1997) *World Orders, Old and New*, London: Pluto; R. Krznaric (2001) 'Mortgaged Democracy' in P. B. Clarke and J. Foweraker (eds.) *Encyclopaedia of Democratic Thought*, London and New York: Routledge: 449–52.

[48] H. Zinn (1995) *A People's History of the United States, 1492 – Present*, New York: HarperPerennial: 255.

[49] M. K. Smith (2001) 'Peter Senge and the Learning Organization'.

[50] P. Senge, O. Scharmer, J. Jaworski, and B. Flowers (2004) *Presence: Human Purpose and the Field of the Future*, Cambridge, MA: Society for Organizational Learning.

[51] See, for instance, some of the change-management tools and exercises at http://www.change-management-toolbook.com.

[52] D. Goleman (1999) *Working With Emotional Intelligence*, London: Bloomsbury: 196–97; M. Kalungu-Banda (2006) *Leading Like Madiba: Leadership Lessons from Nelson Mandela*, Cape Town: Double Storey.

[53] J. Diamond (1998) *Guns, Germs and Steel: A Short History of Everybody for the Last 13,000 Years*, London: Vintage: 406–8.

[54] J. Sachs (2005) *The End of Poverty: How We Can Make It Happen in Our Lifetime*, Harmondsworth, UK: Penguin: 57–9.

[55] S. Bastos and M. Camus (1995) 'Abriendo Caminos: Las organizaciones mayas desde el Nobel hasta el Acuerdo de Derechos Indígenas', Guatemala City: FLACSO.

[56] M. Weber (1968: 180).

[57] C. B. Macpherson (1977) *The Life and Times of Liberal Democracy*, Oxford: Oxford University Press; S. Bowles and H. Gintis (1986).

[58] M. Ruthven (2000) *Islam: A Very Short Introduction*, Oxford: Oxford University Press: Chapter 5.

[59] R. Porter (1997) *The Greatest Benefit to Mankind: A Medical History of Humanity from Antiquity to the Present*, London: HarperCollins: 274–7, 486.

[60] T. Kuhn (1962) *The Structure of Scientific Revolutions*, Chicago: University of Chicago Press: 111–12; 165–6.

[61] B. Russell (1984) *A History of Western Philosophy*, London: Unwin: 111.

[62] D. Howarth (2000) *Discourse*, Buckingham and Philadelphia: Open University Press: 9.

[63] C. R. Adams and M. P. Early (2004) *Principles of Horticulture*, Oxford: Elsevier: 187.

[64] See also the studies of co-operative breeding in birds in Stacey and Koenig (1990).

[65] B. McKibben (1999) *The End of Nature: Humanity, Climate Change and the Natural World*, London: Bloomsbury: 169.

[66] See, for instance, the discussion on 'specialisation and its discontents' in Collini (2006: Chapter 20).

[67] M. Gladwell (2000) *The Tipping Point: How Little Things Can Make a Big Difference*, London: Abacus: 15–29.

[68] T. Zeldin (1995) *An Intimate History of Humanity*, London: Minerva: 326.

[69] Zeldin's ideas have been put into practice through projects such as 'Conversation Meals' run by the foundation he established, The Oxford Muse (see http://www.oxfordmuse.com).

[70] Special thanks to Kate Raworth, Senior Researcher at Oxfam GB, for helping to design and structure the 'rough guide'.

[71] A. Hochschild (2004) 'Against All Odds', *MotherJones*, Jan–Feb.

[72] A. Hochschild (2006) *Bury the Chains: The British Struggle to Abolish Slavery*, London: Pan Books: 127.

[73] A. Hochschild (2006: 67).

[74] A. Hochschild (2006: 95).

[75] A. Hochschild (2006: 129–30; 136).

[76] A. Hochschild (2006: 133).

[77] A. Hochschild (2006: 5).

[78] A. Hochschild (2004).

[79] Of course, slavery, mainly in the form of debt bondage, still exists today in countries such as Brazil, India, and Nepal.

[80] For an analysis of the realities of neo-liberalism in Latin America, see Green (2003).

[81] See, for example, Bhagwati (2005) and Bhagwati and Srinivasan (2002).

[82] M. Khor (2002) 'The WTO, the Post-Doha Agenda and the Future of the Trade System: a development perspective', Penang: Third World Network; Third World Network (December 2001) 'The Multilateral Trading System: A Development Perspective', New York: United Nations Development Programme: 6–16; 79–91; Oxfam (2002) 'Rigged Rules and Double Standards: Trade, Globalisation, and the Fight Against Poverty', Oxford: Oxfam International: 250–57.

[83] AccountAbility (2005) 'Responsible Competitiveness: Reshaping Global Markets Through Responsible Business Practice', London: AccountAbility.

[84] Oxfam (2004) 'Trading Away our Rights: Women Working in Global Supply Chains', Oxford: Oxfam International: 82–5.

[85] ActionAid International (2005) 'Power Hungry: Six Reasons to Regulate Global Food Corporations', London: ActionAid.

[86] On this history of philanthropy see Feingold (1987).

[87] United Nations Conference on Trade and Development (2002) *The Least Developed Countries Report 2002: Escaping the Poverty Trap*, New York and Geneva: United Nations: 214–17; Commonwealth Secretariat (2003) 'Making Democracy Work For Pro-Poor Development: Report by a Commonwealth Group of Experts', London: Commonwealth Secretariat: 52–7.

[88] See Sen (2006) for a review of Easterly's book.

[89] Commonwealth Secretariat (2003: 30).

[90] J. Sachs (2005: 233–4).

[91] See, for example, Center for Economic and Social Rights (1999) and United Nations Development Programme (2000).

[92] For full discussions of the capabilities approach to human development, see Sen (1999: 74–6; Chapter 4); United Nations Development Programme (1990: 9); and Office of the High Commissioner for Human Rights (2002: para.5–6).

[93] N. Kabeer (1999) 'Resources, Agency, Achievements: Reflections on the Measurement of Women's Empowerment', *Development Research and Change* 30(3): 435–64.

[94] R. Chambers (2005) *Ideas for Development*, London: Earthscan: 100–1.

[95] S. P. Jain and W. Polman (2004) *A Handbook for Trainers on Participatory Local Development: The Panchayati Raj model in India*, FAO Regional Office for Asia and the Pacific (Bangkok), second edition.

[96] J. Foweraker and R. Krznaric (2000) 'Measuring Liberal Democratic Performance: An Empirical and Conceptual Critique', *Political Studies* 48(4): 772–3.

[97] R. Chambers (2005: 99).

[98] M. Lockwood (2005) *The State They're In: An Agenda for International Action on Poverty in Africa*, Bourton-on-Dunsmore, UK: ITDG Publishing: Chapters 5–7.

[99] Oxfam (2002: 242–3).

[100] H. De Soto (2000) *The Mystery of Capital: Why Capitalism Triumphs in the West and Fails Everywhere Else*, London: Bantam Press: 7.

[101] N. Kanji (2006) 'Innovation in Securing Land Rights in Africa: Lessons from Experience', London: International Institute of Environment and Development.

[102] C. Sweetman (October 2006) 'How title deeds make sex safer: women's property rights in an era of HIV', internal briefing paper, Oxford: Oxfam GB.

[103] R. Irvine, R. Chambers, and R. Eyben (2004) 'Learning From Poor People's Experience: Immersions', Lessons for Change Series No. 13, University of Sussex: Institute of Development Studies: 6–10.

[104] K. Marx (1954: 23).

References

AccountAbility (2005) 'Responsible Competitiveness: Reshaping Global Markets Through Responsible Business Practice', London: AccountAbility.

ActionAid International (2005) 'Power Hungry: Six Reasons to Regulate Global Food Corporations', London: ActionAid, http://www.actionaid.org/wps/content/documents/power_hungry_222006_1476.pdf, accessed 22 January 2007.

Adams, C. R. and M. P. Early (2004) *Principles of Horticulture*, Oxford: Elsevier.

Adorno, T. and M. Horkenheimer (1997 [1944]) *Dialectic of Enlightenment*, London: Verso.

Anderson, B. (1991) *Imagined Communities: Reflections on the Origin and Spread of Nationalism*, London: Verso.

Bakan, J. (2004) *The Corporation: The Pathological Pursuit of Profit and Power*, London: Constable & Robinson.

Barbalet, J. M. (1995) 'Climates of Fear and Socio-Political Change', *Journal for the Theory of Social Behaviour* 25(1): 15–32.

Barber, E. W. (1994) *Women's Work: The First 20,000 Years: Women, Cloth and Society in Early Times*, New York: W.W. Norton & Company.

Bastos, S. and M. Camus (1995) *Abriendo Caminos: Las organizaciones mayas desde el Nobel hasta el Acuerdo de Derechos Indígenas*, Guatemala City: FLACSO.

Bhagwati, J. (2005) 'From Seattle to Hong Kong: Are We Getting Anywhere?' *Foreign Affairs*, Special Edition, Dec 2005, unedited version, http://www.columbia.edu/~jb38/Bhagwati,%20Foreign%20Affairs.doc, accessed 22 January 2007.

Bhagwati, J. and T. N. Srinivasan (2002) 'Trade and Poverty in Poor Countries', *American Economic Review Papers and Proceedings*, May, http://www.columbia.edu/~jb38/AEA%20Trade%20and%20Poverty%20in%20the%20Poor%20Countries.pdf, accessed 22 January 2007.

Bookchin, M. (1995) *From Urbanization to Cities: Towards a New Politics of Citizenship*, London: Cassell.

Boorstin, D. (1985) *The Discoverers: A History of Man's Search to Know his World and Himself*, New York: Vintage.

Bosignore, J. J., E. Katsh, P. d'Errico, R. M. Pipkin, S. Arons, and J. Rifkin (eds.) (1997) *Before the Law: An Introduction to the Legal Process*, Boston and New York: Houghton Mifflin, 275–7.

Bourdieu, P. (1990) *The Logic of Practice*, Cambridge: Polity.

Bowles, S. and H. Gintis (1986) *Democracy and Capitalism: Property, Community and the Contradictions of Modern Social Thought*, London: Routledge & Kegan Paul.

Buber, M. (1949) *Paths in Utopia*, London: Routledge & Kegan Paul.

Budlender, D. and G. Hewitt (eds.) (2002) *Gender Budgets Make More Cents: Country Studies and Good Practice*, London: Commonwealth Secretariat.

Bull, H. (1977) *The Anarchical Society: A Study of Order in World Politics*, New York: Columbia University Press.

Caldeira, T. (2000) *City of Walls: Crime, Segregation and Citizenship in São Paulo*, Berkeley: University of California Press.

Carlyle, T. (1888 [1845]) *Oliver Cromwell's Letters and Speeches*, London: Chapman and Hall.

Carr, E. H. (1987) *What is History?*, Harmondsworth, UK: Penguin.

Casaus Arzú, M. (1992) *Guatemala: Linaje y Racismo*, San José, Costa Rica: FLASCO.

Castells, M. (1996) *The Rise of the Network Society: The Information Age: Economy, Society and Culture Volume 1*, Cambridge, MA and Oxford: Blackwell.

Center for Economic and Social Rights (1999) 'From Needs to Rights: Realizing the Right to Health in Ecuador', Quito: Centro de Derechos Económicos y Sociales.

Chambers, R. (2005) *Ideas for Development*, London: Earthscan.

Chang, H.-J. (2005) 'Why Developing Countries Need Tariffs: How WTO NAMA Negotiations Could Deny Developing Countries' Right to a Future', South Centre (Geneva), http://www.southcentre.org/publications/SouthPerspectiveSeries/WhyDevCountriesNeedTariffsNew.pdf, accessed 22 January 2007.

Chang, H.-J. (2002) *Kicking Away the Ladder – Development Strategy in Historical Perspective*, London: Anthem Press.

Chomsky, N. (1997) *World Orders, Old and New*, London: Pluto.

Chubb, J. (1982) *Patronage, Power and Poverty in Southern Italy: A Tale of Two Cities*, Cambridge: Cambridge University Press.

Clegg, S. R. (1989) *Frameworks of Power*, London: Sage.

Cohen, S. (2001) *States of Denial: Knowing about Atrocities and Suffering*, Cambridge: Polity Press.

Collini, S. (2006) *Absent Minds: Intellectuals in Britain*, Oxford: Oxford University Press.

Commonwealth Secretariat (2003) 'Making Democracy Work For Pro-Poor Development: Report by a Commonwealth Group of Experts', London: Commonwealth Secretariat.

Dahl, R. A. (1989) *Democracy and its Critics*, New Haven and London: Yale University Press.

Davis, M. (1992) *City of Quartz: Excavating the Future in Los Angeles*, New York: Vintage Books.

Dawkins, R. (1989 [1976]) *The Selfish Gene*, Oxford: Oxford University Press.

De Bono, E. (1970) *Lateral Thinking*, Harmondsworth, UK: Penguin.

De Landa, M. (1997) *A Thousand Years of Nonlinear History*, New York: Zone Books.

Department for International Development (2006) 'Eliminating World Poverty: Making Governance Work for the Poor', UK Department for International Development, http://www.dfid.gov.uk/wp2006/whitepaper-printer-friendly.pdf, accessed 22 January 2007.

De Soto, H. (2000) *The Mystery of Capital: Why Capitalism Triumphs in the West and Fails Everywhere Else*, London: Bantam Press.

Diamond, J. (1998) *Guns, Germs and Steel: A Short History of Everybody for the Last 13,000 Years*, London: Vintage.

Elias, N. and E. Dunning (1986) *Quest For Excitement: Sport and Leisure in the Civilizing Process*, Oxford: Blackwell.

Elson, D. (ed.) (1991) *Male Bias in the Development Process*, Manchester: Manchester University Press.

Fanon, F. (1963) *The Wretched of the Earth*, New York: Grove Press.

Faulks, K. (1998) *Citizenship in Modern Britain*, Edinburgh: Edinburgh University Press.

Feingold, M. (1987) 'Philanthropy, Pomp and Patronage', *Daedalus* 116(1)(Winter): 155–78.

Feyerabend, P. (1975) *Against Method*, London: Verso.

Foley, M. (1991) *American Political Ideas: Traditions and Usages*, Manchester: Manchester University Press.

Foucault, M. (1977) *Discipline and Punish: the Birth of the Prison*, London: Penguin.

Foweraker, J. and R. Krznaric (2002) 'The Uneven Performance of Third Wave Democracies: Electoral Politics and the Imperfect Rule of Law in Latin America', *Latin American Politics and Society* 44(3) (Fall): 29–60.

Foweraker, J. and R. Krznaric (2000) 'Measuring Liberal Democratic Performance: An Empirical and Conceptual Critique', *Political Studies* 48(4): 759–87.

Freud, S. (1996 [1900]) *The Interpretation of Dreams*, New York: Gramercy Books.

Galeano, E. (1982–1986) *Memoria del Fuego*, Madrid: Siglo Veintiuno.

Gaventa, J. (2006) 'Finding the Space for Change: A Power Analysis', *IDS Bulletin: Exploring Power for Change* 37(6)(October).

Geertz, C. (1973) 'Deep Play: Notes on the Balinese Cockfight', in *The Interpretation of Cultures*, London: Fontana: 412–553.

Gibbon, E. (1900 [1788]) *The History of the Decline and Fall of the Roman Empire*, London: Methuen.

Gladwell, M. (2000) *The Tipping Point: How Little Things Can Make a Big Difference*, London: Abacus.

Glassner, B. (2000) *The Culture of Fear: Why Americans are Afraid of the Wrong Things*, New York: Basic Books.

Goleman, D. (1999) *Working With Emotional Intelligence*, London: Bloomsbury.

Goleman, D. (1996) *Emotional Intelligence: Why It Can Matter More Than IQ*, London: Bloomsbury.

Gramsci, A. (1971) *Selections from the Prison Notebooks*, London: Lawrence and Wishart.

Green, D. (2003) *Silent Revolution: The Rise of Market Economics in Latin America*, London: Latin America Bureau.

Hagopian, F. (1996) *Traditional Politics and Regime Change in Brazil*, Cambridge: Cambridge University Press.

Halliday, F. (1994) *Rethinking International Relations*, Basingstoke and London: Macmillan.

Hanh, T. N. (1987) *Being Peace*, London: Rider.

Harvey, D. (1973) *Social Justice and the City*, London: Edward Arnold.

Held, D. (1996) *Models of Democracy*, Cambridge: Polity Press.

Hill, C. (1975) *The World Turned Upside Down: Radical Ideas During the English Revolution*, Harmondsworth, UK: Penguin.

Hobsbawm, E. (1997) *On History*, London: Abacus.

Hobsbawm, E. (1987) *The Age of Empire 1975-1914*, London: Weidenfeld and Nicolson.

Hochschild, A. (2006) *Bury the Chains: The British Struggle to Abolish Slavery*, London: Pan Books.

Hochschild, A. (2004) 'Against All Odds', *MotherJones*, Jan–Feb, http://www.motherjones.com/news/feature/2004/01/12_403.html, accessed 22 January 2007.

Howarth, D. (2000) *Discourse*, Buckingham and Philadelphia: Open University Press.

Huntington, S. (1996) *The Clash of Civilizations and the Remaking of the World Order*, New York: Simon & Schuster.

Irvine, R., R. Chambers, and R. Eyben (2004) 'Learning From Poor People's Experience: Immersions', Lessons for Change Series No. 13, University of Sussex: Institute of Development Studies.

Jain, S. P. and W. Polman (2004) *A Handbook for Trainers on Participatory Local Development: The Panchayati Raj model in India*, FAO Regional Office for Asia and the Pacific (Bangkok), second edition, http://www.fao.org/docrep/006/ad346e/ad346e00.htm#Contents, accessed 22 January 2007.

Johnson, S. (2002) *Emergence: The Connected Lives of Ants, Brains, Cities and Software*, Harmondsworth, UK: Penguin.

Josephson, M. (1962 [1934]) *The Robber Barons: The Great American Capitalists, 1861, 1901*, London: Eyre & Spottiswoode.

Jung, C. (1964) *Man and His Symbols*, London: Picador.

Just Associates, Institute of Development Studies University of Sussex, Knowledge Initiative ActionAid International (2006) 'Making Change Happen: Citizen Engagement and Global Economic Power', http://www.justassociates.org/publications_files/MCH2.pdf, accessed 22 January 2007.

Kabeer, N. (1999) 'Resources, Agency, Achievements: Reflections on the Measurement of Women's Empowerment', *Development and Change* 30(3): 435–64.

Kalungu-Banda, M. (2006) *Leading Like Madiba: Leadership Lessons from Nelson Mandela*, Cape Town: Double Storey.

Kanji, N. (2006) 'Innovation in Securing Land Rights in Africa: Lessons from Experience', London: International Institute of Environment and Development, http://www.iied.org/pubs/display.php? o=12531iied, accessed 22 January 2007.

Keane, J. (ed.) (1988) *Civil Society and the State: New European Perspectives*, London: Verso.

Khor, M. (2002) 'The WTO, the Post-Doha Agenda and the Future of the Trade System: a development perspective', Penang: Third World Network.

Koestler, A. (1964) *The Act of Creation*, London: Hutchinson.

Kohn, A. (1990) *The Brighter Side of Human Nature: Altruism and Empathy in Everyday Life*, New York: Basic Books.

Krog, A. (1998) *Country of My Skull*, London: Jonathan Cape.

Kropotkin, P. (1998 [1902]) *Mutual Aid: A Factor of Evolution*, London: Freedom Press.

Kropotkin, P. (1927 [1886]) 'Law and Authority' in R. N. Baldwin (ed.) *Kropotkin's Revolutionary Pamphlets*, New York: Vanguard Press: 196–218.

Krznaric, R. (2007, forthcoming) *What the Rich Don't Tell the Poor: Conversations in Guatemala*, Guatemala City: Inforpress Centroamericana.

Krznaric, R. (2006) 'The Limits of Pro-poor Agricultural Trade in Guatemala: Land, Labour and Political Power', *Journal of Human Development* 7(1): 111–35.

Krznaric, R. (2003) 'The Worldview of the Oligarchy in Guatemalan Politics', Ph.D. thesis, University of Essex (UK).

Krznaric, R. (2001) 'Mortgaged Democracy' in P. B. Clarke and J. Foweraker (eds.) *Encyclopaedia of Democratic Thought*, London and New York: Routledge: 449–52.

Kubler-Ross, E. (1969) *On Death and Dying*, London: Tavistock Publications.

Kuhn, T. (1962) *The Structure of Scientific Revolutions*, Chicago: University of Chicago Press.

Kymlicka, W. (ed.) (1995) *The Rights of Minority Cultures*, Oxford: Oxford University Press.

Lewis, O. (1961) *The Children of Sanchez: Autobiography of a Mexican Family*, London: Secker and Warburg.

Lijphart, A. (1984) *Democracies: Patterns of Majoritarian and Consensus Government in Twenty-one Countries*, New Haven: Yale University Press.

Lindblom, C. E. (1983) 'The Privileged Position of Business', in M. Green (ed), *The Big Business Reader on Corporate America*, New York: Pilgrim Press: 193–203.

Linz, J. J. and A. Stepan (1996) *Problems of Democratic Transition and Consolidation: Southern Europe, South America, and Post-Communist Europe*, Baltimore and London: Johns Hopkins University Press.

Lockwood, M. (2005) *The State They're In: An Agenda for International Action on Poverty in Africa*, Bourton-on-Dunsmore, UK: ITDG Publishing.

Lovelock, J. (2000) *Gaia: A New Look at Life on Earth*, Oxford: Oxford University Press.

Luxemburg, R. (1986 [1900]) 'Social Reform or Revolution', London: Militant Publications.

Macpherson, C. B. (1977) *The Life and Times of Liberal Democracy*, Oxford: Oxford University Press.

Malthus, T. (1970 [1798]) *An Essay on the Principle of Population*, Harmondswoth, UK: Penguin.

Mann, M. (1993) *The Sources of Social Power, Volume 2: The rise of classes and nation-states, 1760–1914*, Cambridge: Cambridge University Press.

Mannheim, K. (1997 [1952]) *Essays on the Sociology of Knowledge*, London: Routledge.

Marx, K. (1954) *The Eighteenth Brumaire of Louis Bonaparte*, Moscow: Progress Publishers and London: Lawrence and Wishart.

Marx, K. and F. Engels (1974) *The German Ideology*, London: Lawrence and Wishart.

Mayhew, H. (1967 [1851]) *London Labour and the London Poor*, London: Cass.

McKibben, B. (1999) *The End of Nature: Humanity, Climate Change and the Natural World*, London: Bloomsbury.

Miller, W. L. (1995) 'Quantitative Methods', in D. Marsh and G. Stoker (eds.) *Theory and Method in Political Science*, Basingstoke and London: Macmillan: 154–72.

Mills, C. W. (1956) *The Power Elite*, New York: Oxford University Press.

Montesquieu, Charles de Secondat, Baron de (1989 [1748]) *The Spirit of the Laws*, Cambridge: Cambridge University Press.

Moore, B. (1973) *Social Origins of Dictatorship and Democracy: Lord and Peasant in the Making of the Modern World*, Harmondsworth, UK: Penguin University Books.

Mumford, L. (1938) *The Culture of Cities*, New York: Harcourt, Brace and Company.

Narayan, D., R. Patel, K. Schafft, A. Rademacher, and S. Koch-Schulte (2000) *Voices of the Poor: Can Anyone Hear Us?*, Washington: World Bank and New York: Oxford University Press.

O'Donnell, G., P. Schmitter, and L. Whitehead (eds.) (1986) *Transitions From Authoritarian Rule*, Baltimore: Johns Hopkins University Press.

Office of the High Commissioner for Human Rights (2002) 'Draft Guidelines: A Human Rights Approach to Poverty Reduction Strategies', Geneva: Office of the High Commissioner for Human Rights.

Olson, M. (1971) *The Logic of Collective Action: Public Goods and the Theory of Groups*, Harvard: Harvard University Press..

Oxfam (2004) 'Trading Away our Rights: Women Working in Global Supply Chains', Oxford: Oxfam International.

Oxfam (2002) 'Rigged Rules and Double Standards: Trade, Globalisation, and the Fight Against Poverty', Oxford: Oxfam International.

Pinker, S. (2004) 'Why Nature and Nurture Won't Go Away', *Daedalus* Fall: 1–13.

Polanyi, K. (1944) *The Great Transformation: The Political and Economic Origins of Our Time*, Boston: Beacon Press.

Porter, R. (1997) *The Greatest Benefit to Mankind: A Medical History of Humanity from Antiquity to the Present*, London: HarperCollins.

Putnam, R. (1993) *Making Democracy Work: Civic Traditions in Modern Italy*, Princeton, NJ: Princeton University Press.

Rodrik, D. (2004) 'Rethinking Growth Policies in the Developing World', Cambridge MA: Harvard University, http://ksghome.harvard.edu/~drodrik/Luca_d_Agliano_Lecture_Oct_2004.pdf, accessed 22 January 2007.

Rogers, E. M. (1962) *Diffusion of Innovations*, New York: Free Press of Glencoe.

Rueschemeyer, D., E. H. Stephens, and J. D. Stephens (1992) *Capitalist Development and Democracy*, Cambridge: Polity Press.

Russell, B. (1984) *A History of Western Philosophy*, London: Unwin.

Ruthven, M. (2000) *Islam: A Very Short Introduction*, Oxford: Oxford University Press.

Sachs, J. (2005) *The End of Poverty: How We Can Make It Happen in Our Lifetime*, Harmondsworth, UK: Penguin.

Sen, A. (2006) 'The Man Without a Plan', review of William Easterly's *The White Man's Burden: Why the West's Efforts to Aid the Rest Have Done So Much Ill and So Little Good*, in *Foreign Affairs* March/April, http://www.foreignaffairs.org/20060301fareviewessay85214/amartya-sen/the-man-without-a-plan.html, accessed 22 January 2007.

Sen, A. (1999) *Development as Freedom*, New York: Alfred A. Knopf.

Sen, A. (1977) 'Rational Fools: A critique of the behavioural foundations of economic thought', *Philosophy and Public Affairs* 6(4): 317–44.

Senge, P., O. Scharmer, J. Jaworski, and B. Flowers (2004) *Presence: Human Purpose and the Field of the Future*, Cambridge, MA: Society for Organizational Learning.

Senge, P. (1992) *The Fifth Discipline: The Art and Practice of the Learning Organisation*, London: Century Business.

Smith, M. (1995) 'Pluralism', in D. Marsh and G. Stoker (eds.), *Theory and Method in Political Science*, Basingstoke and London: Macmillan: 209–27.

Smith, M. K. (2001) 'Peter Senge and the Learning Organization', http://www.infed.org/thinkers/senge.htm, accessed 22 January 2007.

Stacey, P. and W. Koenig (eds.) (1990) *Cooperative Breeding in Birds*, Cambridge: Cambridge University Press.

Sweetman, C. (October 2006) 'How title deeds make sex safer: women's property rights in an era of HIV', internal briefing paper, Oxford: Oxfam GB.

Terkel, S. (1972) *Working: People Talk About What They Do All Day and How They Feel About What They Do*, New York: Pantheon.

Third World Network (December 2001) 'The Multilateral Trading System: A Development Perspective', New York: United Nations Development Programme.

Thompson, E. P. (1968) *The Making of the English Working Class*, Harmondsworth, UK: Pelican.

United Nations Conference on Trade and Development (2002) *The Least Developed Countries Report 2002: Escaping the Poverty Trap*, New York and Geneva: United Nations.

United Nations Development Programme (2000) *Human Development Report*, New York: Oxford University Press.

United Nations Development Programme (1990) *Human Development Report*, Oxford: Oxford University Press.

Viotti, P. R. and M. V. Kauppi (1993) *International Relations Theory: Realism, Pluralism, Globalism*, New York and Toronto: Macmillan.

Ward, C. (1986) *Anarchy in Action*, London: Freedom Press.

Ward, C. (1979) *The Child in the City*, Harmondsworth, UK: Penguin.

Weatherall, D. (1995) *Science and the Quiet Art: Medical Research and Patient Care*, Oxford: Oxford University Press.

Weber, M. (1968 [1925]) *Economy and Society: An Outline of Interpretive Sociology*, G. Roth and C. Wittich (eds.), New York: Bedminster Press.

Wilson, E. O. (1984) *Biophilia: The human bond with other species*, Harvard, MA: Harvard University Press.

Zeldin, T. (1998) *Conversation*, London: Harvill Press.

Zeldin, T. (1995) *An Intimate History of Humanity*, London: Minerva.

Zinn, H. (1995) *A People's History of the United States, 1492 – Present*, New York: HarperPerennial.

www.ingramcontent.com/pod-product-compliance
Ingram Content Group UK Ltd.
Pitfield, Milton Keynes, MK11 3LW, UK
UKHW050227150426
5217IPUK00023B/1675